ADVANCE PRAISE

"One of the most important pieces of research since Challenger, *The Salesperson's Secret Code* embodies everything that truly professional salespeople would wish to be. The book shows how holding certain beliefs about selling can predict success. For the first time, our 'sales industry' can focus not just on perfecting processes and skills, but also on what causes people to be successful in the first place."

Nick Porter
Chairman of the Association of Professional Sales

"This is not just a book for salespeople. It's a book for everyone. Everyone in every role sells themselves. The authors highlight life skills that encourage us all to be better, more accomplished and more confident humans. A great manual for life."

Michael Tobin OBE
Former CEO at Telecity Group, NED on 4 Continents

"This book is the result of some remarkable research. What the authors have done is to discover the 'difference that makes the difference' between the top salespeople and the rest. And not just a few differences, but many, and some remarkable subtleties. The less busy and the ones who bring fun and legacy into their way of being are the ones who are either the icons or approaching that status. If you want a working text from which to train anyone in the art of influence, this will give you the most comprehensive foundation."

Sue Knight

author of NLP at Work and winner of
the NLP in Business Award 2017

"We know that performance = capability x behaviour. What is one of the primary influencers of behaviour? Beliefs! The secret is out! … in the thoroughly researched, thought-provoking, and rich content of this book."

Adrian Norton

former VP, Global Sales, Indivior plc
(formerly Reckitt Benckiser Pharmaceuticals)

"At last! For someone like me who hires high-end sales professionals, this book has come just in time. Solution selling has become the norm and the market lacks innovation in consequence. *The Salesperson's Secret Code* shows how the best-of-the-best allow the 'real person' to shine through. They walk in the shoes of their customer and, at the same time, have a healthy self-regard – a perfect combination that builds trust. This book adds an array of questioning strategies to use during the selection process and reveal the real 'person behind the sales'."

Laurence Kirk
Sales Director EMEA, Allegis Global Solutions

"Mills, Ridley, Laker and Chapman's research proves what many of us have long known. The very best salespeople are driven to be more, do more, have more, and contribute more. They also want to control their own destiny. You can adopt these beliefs and behaviours, and *the Salesperson's Secret Code* will provide you with the answer key to doing so."

Anthony Iannarino
best-selling author of *The Only Sales Guide You'll Ever Need* and *The Lost Art of Closing: Winning the 10 Commitments That Drive Sales*, and editor of thesalesblog.com.

There are many books out there about what makes a top salesperson successful. However, this book offers a very fresh and insightful analysis on this topic, which will engage readers, enable them to easily take these learnings with them to apply in their daily work and become more successful. Highly recommended for all sales professionals who are serious about upping their game!

Jan Allen

VP, T-systems International GmbH, member of the European Women on Boards association

"*The Salesperson's Secret Code* provides powerful and profound insights into the key beliefs of exceptional sales performers. Essential reading for everyone in the sales profession."

Simon Hazeldine

Best-selling author of *Bare Knuckle Selling, Bare Knuckle Negotiating, Bare Knuckle Customer Service, The Inner Winner*, and *Neuro-Sell: How Neuroscience Can Power Your Sales Success*

"Selling is like a science – it takes both an understanding of theory and a lot of practice to take it to the next level. Sales is the most critical role in any organization and oftentimes the hardest role. You need to be both a leader and a manager to succeed. The insightful analysis in this book make it a valuable resource for all sales executives"

Afi Ofori

Founder of Women in Sales Awards – WISA (Europe, North America and India)

Published by
LID Publishing Limited
The Record Hall, Studio 204,
16-16a Baldwins Gardens,
London EC1N 7RJ, United Kingdom

31 West 34th Street, 8th Floor, Suite 8004,
New York, NY 10001, US

info@lidpublishing.com
www.lidpublishing.com

A member of:

BPR
Business Publishers Roundtable

www.businesspublishersroundtable.com

Printed in Great Britain by TJ International
ISBN: 978-1-911498-00-1

Cover and Page design: Caroline Li

IAN MILLS, MARK RIDLEY, BEN LAKER & TIM CHAPMAN

THE SALESPERSON'S SECRET CODE

THE BELIEF SYSTEMS THAT DISTINGUISH WINNERS

LONDON   MONTERREY
MADRID   SHANGHAI
MEXICO CITY   BOGOTA
NEW YORK   BUENOS AIRES
BARCELONA   SAN FRANCISCO

CONTENTS

"*Act as if what you do makes a difference. It does. Be not afraid of life. Believe that life is worth living, and your belief will help create the fact.*"

William James,
Father of American Psychology,
1842–1910

ACKNOWLEDGEMENTS

The authors would like to thank the following for their unstinting support. Without you this book could not have become a reality.

Two of our fellow partners at Transform Performance International:

- Nancy Loates-Taylor, who has provided valuable ideas and thought leadership.
- Tanya Lucas, who has provided the psychology professional's perspective and is the embodiment of everything we have written about, having been declared the "Best Woman in Professional Services Sales" at the Women in Sales Awards (Europe), 2016.

All the staff at Transform Performance International, who have kept us organized throughout.

Sam Chapman, for his hours spent transcribing interview after interview.

Nic Read, for his invaluable assistance during the editing process.

Our "Iconic" salespeople, the businesses that allowed us access to their salespeople, and the salespeople themselves who allowed us into their very personal worlds.

Our publisher, LID, for believing in the project and for its support in delivering the published work.

FOREWORD 1

We are entering a period of change and uncertainty in politics, culture and business. In this climate, companies are increasingly looking to their salespeople to make the difference. But sales isn't only about business. We all sell, every day. Across countries and cultures, industries and age groups, selling is persuasion. In The Salesperson's Secret Code, the researchers have put hard data and cold facts above the imprecisions and vague descriptions that normally surround the subject. Some of the world's most successful salespeople describe the mindset that allowed them to keep on selling around the globe, across different industries and through good times and bad. Perhaps for the first time, the inner life of the salesperson is given equal attention to their outer life, revealing the beliefs and systems of thinking that together bring about the kind of person who outsells the competition time and time again. From learning what a chicken farm can teach you about body language to discovering the connection between bodybuilding and sales fatigue, there is something for everyone to glean from every read. The insights found in this book, and the skill and persuasiveness with which it is written, make The Salesperson's Secret Code not solely the latest offering on the subject, but essential reading. If you want to close more deals – in life or in business – this is the book to help you win.

Luke Johnson
Chairman of Risk Capital Partners LLP and former Chairman of Channel 4 Television, Luke Johnson writes a weekly column for *The Sunday Times* and is part-owner of Patisserie Holdings, Bread Ltd (the firm behind the Gail's Artisan Bakery chain.) He is also Chairman and majority owner of Neilson Active Holidays and serves on the board of sporting goods company Zoggs, Brompton Bicycles and Gaucho Restaurants. He is the largest shareholder and a director of Elegant Hotels Group plc, the largest hotel business in Barbados.

FOREWORD 2

Almost every mission-critical function of a company has standards of compliance. To work in finance, engineering, legal, manufacturing or distribution, workers must study prescribed texts, pass exams, be accredited and then maintain ongoing certification. To some extent the same is true for marketing and customer service operators.

These qualifications came in handy following the 2008 financial crisis, as leaders sought good advice from their lieutenants to trim costs and preserve profit. With those cuts made there's little fat left to trim from the bottom line anymore. Now profit needs to be created by lifting the top line. This makes the business process of selling absolutely mission-critical. More than ever, it puts the sales department in the crosshairs for executive scrutiny.

Yet when you lift the lid, selling isn't really a profession. Not yet. There are no prescribed texts or exams, no official qualifications nor ongoing recertification. It's a career with a low barrier to entry that remains largely unregulated in an age brimming with compliance standards for almost everything else.

Sooner or later, the various standards offices and auditors will be searching for foundational texts to help them demystify selling and put frameworks in place. They'll want to turn sales into a more predictable, repeatable science to reduce the volatility of revenue forecasts and pipeline reviews.

The Salesperson's Secret Code is destined to help.

It's based on real research with iconic salespeople who have outsold, outperformed and outpaced their rivals for the majority of their careers, through boom and bust cycles, in every season. Their insights are gold.

The researchers applied rigour to their approach, collating data from a wide array of salespeople across industries, cultures and geographies. The variety, depth of investigation and quality of interpretation make this book a welcome addition to any sales library.

Perhaps this book's most meaningful contribution is that it reveals for the first time the five beliefs held by every top seller in the world. In an industry brimming with software, templates, methodologies and buzzwords, the inner belief systems of high performers have rarely been explored, and are most welcome.

It shows that achieving excellence is a personal choice, and that lasting change is best achieved from the inside out, rather than being imposed from the outside in. As such, it's a touchstone you can return to multiple times and find something new on each visit. When you read it again, and it feels like the first time, it won't be that the nature of this book has changed between readings, but that your ability to see its gems has grown with each new experience.

Nicholas A. C. Read

Author of *Selling to the C suite*, Nic Read is a researcher and bestselling sales author, who was formerly Executive Director of Ernst & Young's revenue growth advisory practice following a career in sales and management. His methods have been deployed in more than 40 countries, helping clients win billions of dollars above expectation.

CHAPTER ONE

DISCOVERING THE SALESPERSON'S SECRET CODE

In 2013 we (researchers Mark Ridley and Ian Mills) were asked to improve sales results at a global telecommunications company. There we met Tim Chapman, who was responsible for developing and running a sales excellence programme for 750 sales managers and account managers across North America, Europe, Middle East & Africa and Asia-Pacific. Both he and his company wanted to know if good salespeople are born or made, and what motivates high performance.

After surveying staff, conducting joint customer visits and interviewing leaders inside the business, we wondered how the trends being uncovered compared to those across the wider sales profession.

We turned to Dr Ben Laker, an academic from the Centre for High Performance, to build a broader academic study capable of yielding cross-industry, empirical evidence to answer that question. He invited 5,000 organizations across primary, secondary and tertiary sectors – many of whom have a global footprint – to become research partners.

Each organization was asked to nominate a cross-section of ten salespeople. This created a list of 50,000 respondents, but rather than ask their bosses who the high or low performers were, we ran our own independent analysis across multiple factors (not solely based on revenue contribution) to remove bias and increase reliability. On our scorecard, we calculated a median, and people ranked north or south of that marker. This created two groups based on performance. Then, we took the 500 highest-performing respondents from Group 1 and the 500 lowest-performing respondents from Group 2. This provided a 'petri dish' of 1,000 respondents to magnify under our microscope. It is worth saying at this point that when we refer to 'High' and 'Low' performers we are, therefore, talking in relative terms. It does not follow that all low-performers are poor salespeople. They may well be delivering on target for their respective organizations. What we do know, however, is that in comparison with others in our petri dish, for one reason or another, they do not perform as effectively.

The groups were surveyed on what really motivates them to choose and stay in a sales career where they work long hours, face the relentless pressure of appraisal against sales metrics, deal with rejection and politics, and spend so much time away from home. There's an old-fashioned stereotype that says salespeople are all motivated by money. That turns out to be true to some extent, but it's not their biggest motivator, and is only one factor in a multi-dimensional set of drivers. Then, an assessment was completed on every salesperson by our Transform Performance psychometricians (professionals in the study of educational or psychological measurements) to delve into their motivation on a deeper level. You can read more detail about this assessment in Appendix A – Alignment to 6 Attitudes.

Our work in 2013 raised more questions about the mind-set of successful salespeople than it answered. We concluded that we had some insight, but we had not found any identifiable patterns; nothing that led us to think that there was any kind of 'operating system' for the most successful salespeople that the rest of us could potentially model for ourselves. Of course, we might have been searching for the crock of gold at the end of the rainbow. We may have been looking for something that simply did not exist; but our instincts told us otherwise.

In 2015 the research team decided to dig deeper. Each of the 1,000 salespeople was interviewed for 90 minutes about their turn-ons, turn-offs, ambitions and attitudes toward selling. Questions were semi-structured in format. By this we mean that we asked very open 'starter' questions, which invited the interviewee to respond in whatever way they liked. Our interviewers then used a technique known as 'clean questioning' to explore in depth how each salesperson was interpreting their own sales world and how they used their experiences to create a structure for their own success. All answers were recorded and transcribed. The resulting transcripts were analysed using data and language analysis software, through which commonly repeated key words and ideas were isolated.

Now things were becoming exciting. This latest exercise revealed five core, or foundational, beliefs held by all the salespeople we interviewed. After some consideration, we decided to call these five beliefs *Destination Beliefs*. This is because many of those interviewed regard their professional (and personal) life as an ever-expanding journey. Though they acknowledged the importance of the belief in shaping their mind-sets and behaviours, they repeatedly pointed out that these core beliefs are aspirational, evolving continuously, and certainly not finite. Destination Beliefs, we concluded, embody a single, over-arching truth: that beliefs are matters of personal "faith" and will flex and change along with one's life experience.

The five Destination Beliefs were given names and explored through further interviews (*see Figure 1*). We included in these interviews ten of the world's most successful salespeople, whom we called 'The Iconics'. You can learn about them at the end of this chapter.

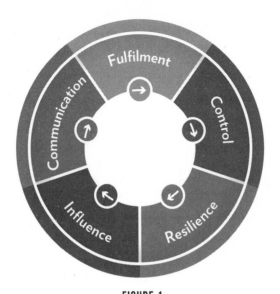

FIGURE 1
INTERCONNECTEDNESS OF THE 5 DESTINATION BELIEFS THAT UNDERPIN
THE SALESPERSON'S SECRET CODE

The most exciting insight from our research was that all salespeople, without exception, referenced most of the five Destination Beliefs during our interview. Everyone could offer detailed stories about almost daily occurrences where the belief drove a motivation, which prompted a behaviour, that achieved a result. Think about that for a moment. From top performers to low performers there was recognition of what made them feel fulfilled, for example, or what being resilient meant to them. But this was not the whole story. It was clear that the Destination Beliefs are necessary components of a salesperson's belief system, but what really separated the top performers from the lower performers was how those beliefs were interpreted and synthesized internally. Put simply, for each Destination Belief our interviewees described a wide array of attitudes towards the belief. These were the ten sub-beliefs. We will explore the precise nature of the spectrum of sub-beliefs, but what is most interesting is that many interviewees experience and even wrestle internally with sub-beliefs from either end, or both ends, of the spectrum. What we learned is that the most successful salespeople respond to certain sub-beliefs with *greater intensity* than they do to others. And it is their response to the intensity of the sub-belief which motivates them to behave in a particular way. For this reason, we have called the sub-beliefs *Journey Motivators*. Journey Motivators send us down a particular track; they demonstrate how we respond to what happens to us on the journey. Journey Motivators set our attitude, and when we use the word "attitude" here, we do not mean a good or bad attitude (although if the cap fits…). What we mean by attitude here is the original dictionary definition, where one takes a perspective, standpoint, position or approach. As leadership expert John Maxwell says, your attitude is "the librarian of your past, the speaker of your present and the prophet of your future." Journey Motivators lay out in front of us the path that we will walk. And though much may have been said and written about having the "right kind of attitude", now, for the first time, we can measure it in a specific population. Here, finally, is a causal chain, a formula for success – *The Salesperson's Secret Code*.

The implications for sales leaders are huge. The standard interview question that elicits the expected response about "hard work" leading to success is no longer good enough. Frankly, such questions should now be considered lazy. All salespeople recognize that hard work matters; it's just that some respond to the challenge of hard work differently because of the way they respond to the intensity of the Journey Motivators they hold.

How did these Journey Motivators manifest themselves? In summary, top-performers believe in giving themselves permission to be better than they ever dreamed possible. Conversely, low-performers believe that success comes from avoiding failure. Top-performers hold themselves accountable for their success; low-performers are happier to attribute lack of success to factors they perceive to be outside of their control. Those in the highest-performing group look for ways to work *smarter* when facing tough times; the lower-performers talk about working *harder*. High achievers know that having influence comes through demonstrating flexibility, not brute force associated with position or power. And finally, the top-performing salespeople regard communication as an ever-deepening dialogue, whereas lower performers tend to view communication as more transactional and transmission-centric.

Armed with this insight, when recruiting in the future, sales leaders will be far better equipped to investigate the deeper motivations and beliefs that drive the best-of-the-best.

Let's explore the five Destination Beliefs. Thereafter, a chapter will be dedicated to each of them and the relative intensity of the Journey Motivators explored to reveal the optimal balance in top-performers: The Salesperson's Secret Code.

Fulfilment is the first component. It's a state of satisfaction that comes from knowing you've either achieved, or are on track to shift performance from good, to better, to best. High-performers are constantly evaluating themselves against a personal progress goal to be the most professional, productive salesperson they can be. They know the extent to which a potential customer engages with them is a reflection of their personal style of communication (more on this later), credibility and persuasiveness.

High-performers understand the concept of ***Control***, the second element. They believe in having a plan, and regularly evaluate where they want to be, where they are, and what the gap is. They show a sense of personal accountability for their success or failure. When fail-

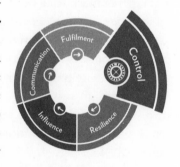

ure comes (and yes, it does even for top performers), they don't blame the economy, their company or the marketing department. They embrace it and take ownership of it, because when you own a problem you can do something to change it. Failure is therefore seen as a temporary setback on the road to inevitable success, where every mile of asphalt, every pothole, every bridge, tollgate and detour is seen as something you can control.

Resilience comes next. It is connected to Control in that it represents your ability to bounce back from setbacks and get back on track. Like Control, Resilience is revealed through taking action. Like a muscle that grows after exercise, or a chunk of coal that gains value after being squeezed under pressure, resilient salespeople face whatever the world throws at them, convert the stress to positive energy, and get busy shaping their own destiny. Resilience means being adaptable to change, and showing a "can do" approach when the pressure is on to meet deadlines, advance the sale, win the deal and hit quota. Resilience is a fundamental building block for achieving influence as a salesperson.

Influence is the fourth piece in this jigsaw puzzle. As a sales professional, you need to gain influence with people in the customer's organization to open doors, get on the calendar, gain stakeholder support and win business. You also need influence with people in your

own company to secure resources, sales support or the pricing needed to close specific deals. You need influence to plug in to the internal grapevine and know about changes, risks or opportunities before they're general knowledge. Some people characterize this type of behaviour as political

– and they're right. You will always encounter politics on the job. People will always be jockeying to be noticed, gain allies, build a power base or exert influence over their work environment. It requires extra effort to navigate this, which is why resilience provides such a vital foundation. Influence is gained by networking, talking to a lot of people, and using the wisdom of crowds to your advantage so you're never caught by surprise. When you know in advance what changes are coming, how people feel about them, what they most want, and whose opinion really matters, you can take action faster and more precisely than others. You build a track record of success. You gain partisans and friends in all the right places. This gives you influence. A key building block to doing all this is your ability to communicate.

Communication is the fifth piece of the puzzle. You can never over-communicate with your colleagues or with a customer. Speed and clarity are key. Speed is important because today people ingest and send information in person, or by

phone, video, email, blog and tweet. If you can't say it in 200 characters or less, some people switch off. So instead of long meetings, letters or emails every few weeks, try having shorter exchanges every few days. The important thing is to stay front-of-mind. Clarity is important; there's so much noise competing for people's attention that your message needs to be precise and cut through the static. Try thinking of every communication as a three-part story: you need an attention-grabbing headline, a reason it matters, and a call to action. This applies to what you write and what you say. The lesson we took from the interview analysis was clear: high performers *think* about how they communicate. They recognize that communication is never a matter of one-size-fits-all. In short, they are flexible, chameleon-like. And they are like this because they come from a place where they believe that they have a duty to help others understand, to enable the asking of questions – in short, to generate dialogue.

Before we go any further, let's address the question of gender. Did we uncover any evidence in our study that males and females hold different beliefs, or at least differing *intensity* of Journey Motivators? The short answer is no, we did not. When we set up the project and approached many organizations we asked them to provide data concerning their top and lower performers. We did not ask them to provide specific numbers on which were male or female. We may have gathered feedback from industries that remain male-dominated. We may have spoken with certain sectors where women predominate. We were not focusing on gender for our study (although we may well address this in future surveys). We simply wished to ascertain the belief systems of those who are already on the job and selling to earn their living. We made no judgment about who is in a particular role, let alone what sex they are. When we analysed our data, we discovered that we had interviewed 65% male and 35% female in the wider "whole group" survey. When we narrowed down our top-performing salespeople, an analysis of the gender split revealed 69% male and 31% female. We excluded our super-achieving Iconics from this figure, since we deliberately chose to balance the sexes when making our selection. The fact that the ratio of males to females remains consistent between the wider group and the top-performing group may be telling, or it may be purely coincidental. We are unable to draw conclusions at this juncture, but it's one fascinating project for the future. Watch this space!

So, let's summarize where we are so far:

- Salespeople spend their lives on a journey towards objectives, sales goals and sales targets – it's in their DNA. Our research concluded that all salespeople hold 5 universal beliefs, which we termed 'Destination Beliefs'. They are fulfilment, control, resilience, influence and communication.
- The more fulfilled and confident you become, the more gravitas you project, and the more *control* you exert over your environment.
- The more in-control you are, the more easily you evade obstacles. But even when you can't, you deal with challenges in a way that builds your emotional, mental or spiritual muscles – your *resilience*.
- The more resilient you are, the more you choose to act rather than be acted upon; the more people and events you will *influence*.
- The more influence you gain, the more doors open to connect you with other influencers. You become better informed, hear of opportunities before others, and greatly improve the quality of your *communication* with others.
- The better your *communication*, the more conversations and ideas you explore with people, and the more opportunities you can uncover to pursue your personal goals for *fulfilment*.
- And the more fulfilled and confident you become, the more gravitas you project ... and so on.

The routes that salespeople take on the journey towards their destination are different. And it's the route they take that defines their sales performance. Our research identified that what separates top performers from the lower performers is how those destination beliefs are interpreted and synthesized internally. For each Destination Belief we identified a spectrum of attitudes towards that belief. These are the "Journey Motivators'. There are ten Journey Motivators, one at each end of the spectrum for each Destination Belief. The top 5% of salespeople have been plotted on the journey motivators spectrum for each Destination Belief and it is the precise balance of motivations for each Destination Belief which reveals the Salesperson's Secret Code. The Salesperson's Secret Code is a self-actualizing, self-supporting *cycle* of behaviour and beliefs, used by every one of the Iconics who shared their insights with us. We'd like to introduce you to them.

THE ICONICS

According to the US Bureau of Labor Statistics, one in nine Americans works in sales. Every day more than 15 million people earn their keep by persuading someone else to make a purchase. But dig deeper and a startling truth emerges. Yes, one in nine Americans works in sales. But so do the other eight, according to Daniel Pink. The former Al Gore speechwriter suggests that whether we're employees pitching colleagues on a new idea, entrepreneurs enticing funders to invest, or parents and teachers cajoling children to study, we spend our days trying to move others. It's no longer about the *ABC of selling* ('Always Be Closing'). Selling is not limited to call centres, shops or garage forecourts. It's something we all do every day – when we try and convince our children to go to bed, we are 'moving' them to get what we want, in the same way as we might persuade someone to purchase a loaf of artisanal bread. Like it or not, we're all in sales now, because to sell is to be human.

For this reason, we selected ten 'iconic' individuals from a diverse range of backgrounds, with different experiences and narratives. We were attracted to them not just because they slammed their sales targets in their particular field, but because we were led to them via others who held them up as special, different, having a certain 'je ne sais quoi' that no one could quite put their finger on. In short, they hold belief systems that distinguish them as winners and have become the embodiment of The Salesperson's Secret Code. Some are senior sales leaders, some are now business leaders and some are salespeople. Some are at the end of their career and some are on their way up. What binds them together is that they have all engaged in business development in its multiplicity of forms and are passionate about its significance. So, in that vein, let us take a closer, personal look at our 'Iconics'.

CHUCK POL,
FORMERLY OF VODAFONE

Chuck Pol has more than 30 years of experience in the global telecommunications industry, with a consistent track record of turning around under-performing businesses and leading teams to dig deep and over-achieve during periods of turbulence and uncertainty.

He chaired the Vodafone US Board of Directors, was chairman of the Vodafone Foundation, and was also Americas President of Vodafone Global Enterprise. Chuck joined Vodafone in 2010 after a 20-year career at British Telecom, where he served in executive roles in the Americas and Europe in sectors that included Mobile, Wholesale and Global Financial Services.

A graduate of Belmont Abbey College, where he is now giving back as a Non-Executive Director, Chuck is married with three grown children.

We asked Chuck, "What does a high performer look like to you?" He replied, "They're available to the client – the one who delivers on their promises, listens effectively, and is always prepared because they do their homework to know what they're talking about. They take the right people with them into any meeting, and don't pretend to be somebody they're not – while they're able to adjust their style, they're still true to themselves. Of course, they also follow up, follow up, and follow up!"

When asked, "What do you want people to learn from your experience?" he answered, "To be prepared to step up and lead in good and bad times, and handle the management of change. It's important to engage with people and create trust by delivering what you say you will to customers, and also up, down and sideways to people in your own company."

COLLEEN SCHULLER, GLAXOSMITHKLINE

After graduating from California Polytechnic University, Colleen Schuller began her career as an Account Executive at Sebastian International, a global hair care and cosmetics company. She rose to Divisional Sales Manager and achieved record growth before accepting a

Pharmaceutical Representative role with GlaxoSmith-Kline Pharmaceuticals in 2000. A stellar track record saw her promoted to Vice President of Sales for 800 professionals selling to the US cardiovascular, metabolic and urology therapy markets. Now Vice President and Global Head of Selling Excellence, Colleen is responsible for setting standards for GSK's global sales force.

Her distinctiveness resides in her ability to lead and motivate people, both in a team setting and on a one-on-one basis. She brings energy and passion to her work, as well as high expectations for the people around her. Now based in London with her husband John and two sons, she enjoys international travel, outdoor adventures and spending time with friends and family.

We asked, "What do you want people to learn from your experience?" Here's what Colleen told us: "Fast-forward the tape five years and really think about what you want to be known for. Are you doing your job because you love it, and making the most of it? What is the mark you want to make, and if you can't do it where you are, will you take action to find a role you can thrive in? Be a learner, as well as a role model to others. To not be sharing, learning and growing would be a real miss. Is your character really shining through? When you're your authentic self, you will always be more successful."

"What does a high performer look like to you?" we asked. "You're competitive," she said. "You take pride in exceeding your targets and increase market share faster than the competition. You are customer-focused to the point that they're letting you through the door, but stone-walling your competitors. This is a huge clue that you're the one adding the most value."

ERICA FEIDNER,
STEINWAY

In 2011, *Inc.* magazine named Erica Feidner one of the ten greatest salespeople of all time, an exclusive list that includes Larry Ellison, David Ogilvy, Dale Carnegie and Zig Ziglar. Erica grew up in a house with 30 pianos, began playing at age three and was teaching adults by the age of nine. She earned a scholarship to New York's prestigious Juilliard School of Music and made her solo orchestral debut at age 11. Erica put herself through college to earn her

Bachelor of Fine Arts degree, and wondered how she could afford her own grand piano. An advertisement for the Miss America pageant offered prize money, so she entered, and won a talent scholarship that allowed her to purchase her first Steinway with the winnings.

When a skiing accident damaged her hand, and left her unable to play to the exacting professional standards she demands of herself, Erica offered to work at Steinway Hall, matching customers to the right piano. She became Steinway's top representative in the world for a decade, during which time she broke all records. Her novel approach to finding the perfect piano for each client earned her the title The Piano Matchmaker™, and she was featured in a story in *The New Yorker* by Pulitzer Prize-winning journalist James B. Stewart. Erica now runs her own company in this field.

We asked, "What do you want people to learn from your experience?" Erica told us, "I don't sell pianos. I sell inspiration. I touch people's lives with the idea that there's one remarkable piano waiting for them, and they can fill their home with music for the rest of their lives. So, I want them to walk out with a real diamond. When you focus on what's right for each customer, the dynamic shifts. You don't sell a product to them; they buy an experience from you."

We asked Erica, "What does a high performer look like to you?" "Don't make it about quota, or your needs," she said. "It's about the customer, and their needs. If I have several pianos that are a close fit, but not the perfect one, I'll turn down the opportunity, and ask them for time to go find the exact solution. Customers are always delighted. The point is to do the right thing, every single time. It's about integrity. You build a personal reputation, fiercely defend it, and customers won't deal with anyone but you."

LOUIS JORDAN, FORMERLY OF DELOITTE & KPMG

Louis Jordan retired recently after spending 16 years as a Partner and Vice Chairman of the professional services firm, Deloitte. During that time he held a number of senior management and lead client roles in the firm, both in the UK and globally. He oversaw the implementation of several innovative market initiatives and was personally responsible for developing and leading some of the firm's largest client relationships.

Prior to this, Louis was a Partner at KPMG, specializing in the Banking and Insurance sectors, primarily in the UK, US and Switzerland. While at KPMG, Louis developed and built the firm's capability to support Financial Sector clients through operational transformation and post-merger integration.

Before entering the world of work, Louis graduated in Economics and Modern History from Manchester University.

We asked, "What do you want people to learn from your experience?" His response: "Be in business with your client; seek to align your interests. Look for a commonality of purpose, where the combination of joint capabilities produces far more than either could on their own. Measure how you have added value to each other through your relationship and continue to build on these positives."

When asked "What does a high performer look like to you?" he answered, "They are utterly reliable and always deliver to the client need. They balance intellect and emotional intelligence, form lasting commercial relationships that transcend individual transactions, and they put the full power of their organization at the disposal of the client."

DILIP MAILVAGANAM,
MICROSOFT

Dilip Mailvaganam studied Computer Science at Reading
University in England and began his career as a software

developer and trainer in an Oxfordshire startup. Assignments in training, consulting, sales and management were a prelude to his being appointed UK General Manager for an offshore services company, which was later acquired by Cognizant.

He joined Microsoft in 2008 to grow European sales for a new offshore services division. By the time he was finished, revenue had grown a staggering 27 times over, and he was appointed Global Delivery Sales Director for Europe Middle East & Africa and Asia-Pacific . He is presently Worldwide Business Development Director, Microsoft Services Emerging Capabilities.

Dilip now lives in London with his wife and two daughters. In his downtime he enjoys rugby, skiing and motor racing.

"What do you want people to learn from your experience," we asked. "You should try to work with as many different people as you can, and not try to do it all yourself," Dilip said. "If you don't have a network, go build one. Work collaboratively inside your own company, and inside your customer's company. There should be no distinction between the two. Customers need to regard you as an indispensable part of their business, or you risk being replaced."

We asked Dilip, "What does a high performer look like to you?" He told us, "Today it's no longer just about making revenue. It's about knowing what impact you're having on your customer's business. Never sell and then walk away. All you've done at that stage is make promises. The selling really starts *after* you have sealed the deal. High-performers make sure they win and keep customers for life."

JUSTIN STONE,
FORMERLY OF J. P. MORGAN

Justin Stone grew up in West Wales with little money and an incomplete education, and was a penniless drifter until he met his future wife and found new purpose. His career gateway was the British Army, from which he joined the AXA Direct call centre in Essex, England. There he applied military discipline to break the process of selling down into replicable component steps and execute with peak efficiency. He quickly became the top seller and was promoted to team leader.

Three years later Justin was admitted to Henderson Global Investors as a Client Services Team Manager in the City, London's financial centre. A role with The Hartford, a US firm entering the UK market, prepared him for a national role with Aegon four years later.

Attending to his education along the way, in 2011 Justin was elevated to head of Schroders' national sales desk, where he found he had a knack for applying advanced analytics to the improvement of sales practices across the asset management firm. In 2014 Justin was invited to assume a role at J. P. Morgan as Vice President leading the company's UK Field Sales Executives in Asset Management.

We asked Justin, "What do you want people to learn from your experience?" This is what he told us: "When I see salespeople being very busy, I know it means they're not being as effective as they could be. Some point to their high sales and say 'I'm hammering it!' But if you want to play the long game, you need to break your week down to the hour, and make sure you're acting, not reacting. Less is more. It has taken me years to understand this, but when you do it, you see massive improvements."

We asked Justin, "What does a high performer look like to you?" "You're the sort of person who watches what the number-one person does," he said. "You're always finding ways to hone your craft. Look at Disneyland – every small thing matters. Attention to detail is crucial. My point is, make sure everything you do is first rate, especially if it's something the customer values."

PHIL BENTON,
ADIDAS

Phil Benton started his sales career as a territory manager in the food and beverage industry for Scottish & Newcastle Breweries. He joined Europe's largest sportswear manufacturer, Adidas, in 1994 and rose through an array of sales and management assignments across retail, trade and account marketing, helping the Adidas and Reebok brands go up against such competitors as Nike, New Balance, Asics and Under Armour. In 2012 he was appointed Sales Director and hand-picked to lead the Adidas partnership with the London Olympic Games. Adidas provided official London 2012 apparel and merchandise, plus gear for Team Great Britain and 3 million items of clothing for volunteers and athletes in the Olympic Village. Phil's team helped the company achieve a record year, with sales of licensed products exceeding $130 million (USD), more than triple what Adidas garnered from the Beijing Olympics. Phil has since been promoted to Vice President, UK & Ireland.

A native of Nottingham, England Phil studied at the University of the West of England, then the University of Birmingham. He is now settled in the northwest of England with his wife and three children, and is a lifelong Norwich City Football Club supporter. He also coaches field hockey after playing for eight years in the National League.

"What do you want people to learn from your experience," we asked. Phil told us: "Build yourself a culture of not wanting to fail, but learn to embrace the reality that some things will go wrong. Learn from both. The sales environment is entrepreneurial by nature, so even if you have processes and strategies as guides, be prepared to innovate, and pivot to where customers want to go."

We asked Phil, "What does a high performer look like to you?" He responded: "High performers are the quiet achievers who just get on with the job and deliver. You can count on them to come through for the team. When you hear people bragging about what they're about to do, or even what they've just done, they're usually the insecure ones still trying to prove themselves. High performers know their worth, and project a vibe of humility, confidence and gravitas. They have a plan for their work activities, and a plan for their private life, and manage both like a boss."

CLAIRE EDMONDS,
CLARIFY

In 2003 Claire Edmunds used the arrival of her first child as a springboard for setting up her own sales business to exploit a marketplace gap she'd spotted. She set up Clarify, a specialist business development company, offering a fundamentally different operating model for enterprise sales – one that delivers predictable pipeline and revenue but also creates long-term transformational change. Fear of failure was a concern for Claire, who spoke of junior managers who were often worried about taking on additional responsibilities: "They are nervous about doing things wrong, so fear of failure becomes an inhibitor. Once people are given the encouragement to take risks and they give themselves permission to make mistakes, they can fly." Claire persevered, and her mission is to change the way that companies use and value business development. Through organic growth, Clarify now delivers value to a global client base of famous-name companies and has a multi-million-dollar turnover. She says that success is down to managers and mentors: "You need people around you to push you to take a risk, to try something different. In some environments, it's hard for many women to raise their hand and say with certainty that they can do something. Men seem to have so much more blind faith in their own abilities!"

Before founding Clarify, Claire worked in marketing and fundraising. In 2014 she was named *The Business Magazine's* "Woman of the Year" (SME), which celebrates women who have achieved significant results and excellence in their field. In June 2015 she was recognized by *Real Business Magazine* and the business advocacy group CBI as "First Woman of Business Services" at the national First Women in Business awards, which celebrate the contributions of female business leaders across the UK. She lives in West Hampshire with her husband and four children, who keep her weekends hectic with a very demanding sporting calendar!

We asked Claire, "What does a high performer look like to you?" "Someone who is hungry to do the right thing," was her response. "They need to be able to investigate and drill into a problem or challenge. They are able to open the customer conversation to consider the long-term perspective."

"What do you want people to learn from your experience?" we asked. Claire told us: "Being able to maintain momentum is very important. In other words, keep things moving by pushing and ensuring they understand which gear the customer needs to be in at different times."

HARRIET TAYLOR,
FORMERLY OF ORACLE

Harriet Taylor worked in the Customer Relationship Management (CRM) stream at Oracle, a software company. Her clients included global corporations and national governments. She is not your typical salesperson. In fact, there is nothing typical about her.

She's part scientist, part musician, part JavaScript queen, and was responsible for ensuring that Oracle sold the very best integrated CRM solutions, breaking down silos and delivering a seamless customer experience across marketing, sales, commerce, service and social, as well as the roles that configure, price and quote.

Before joining Oracle, Harriet graduated from the University of Kent, England, with a first-class honours degree in Physics. Her knowledge of theoretical physics was so substantial she was awarded the school's Physics Project Prize for an outstanding contribution to the field. Before university she studied the flute at Trinity College London and achieved a Grade 8 Distinction. Harriet lives in Kent with her husband, a chartered accountant, and their miniature schnauzer Jake. When she's not working, she is pumping iron at the local gym.

We asked Harriet, "What do you want people to learn from your experience?" She replied: "I am trying to be the best I can be and I would want that of you too. One of my frustrations in life is that I don't know as many people that are quite as driven as me, and I wonder what's wrong with them. If you really push yourself to *work smart*, you will achieve great things that you never thought were possible."

"What does a high performer look like to you?" we asked. Harriet's response: "You aren't afraid to fail (which the psychologists say is essentially all about fearing yourself). It is irrational to fear yourself. If you can recognize that, you find it's okay to fail. Obviously, every success is important, but you still probably haven't achieved the best you're capable of. Unless you tell yourself you've already peaked, you can keep improving forever. I certainly plan to. A real professional is someone who reaches the top of their game, stays humble, keeps learning, finds a higher mountain to climb, and takes others with them."

IRIS SCHOENMAKERS,
CISCO SYSTEMS

After successful roles working for Sony, Madame Tussaud's
and a Formula One racing team, Iris Schoenmakers struck

out to launch companies in the Netherlands and Germany. Her enterprises included two interpretation agencies, an upscale perfume design studio and the international branch of a Swedish HR IT company. In 2011 she was headhunted by Cisco Systems (EMEA–Russia) to focus on improving channel productivity, managing the psychology of behavioural change, and driving sales improvement across multiple cultures and borders in virtual teams. This was a challenge because she was part of a matrixed system with no direct line authority. Iris had to master the art of diplomacy and influence, very quickly. She now works across a portfolio of Cisco's larger technology and services partners, each with a minimum annual spend of $30 million, where Iris and her team are responsible for retaining and building each strategic relationship.

When we asked Iris "What do you want people to learn from your experience?" she told us: "Try different things; explore who you are as a professional, what comes natural to you and what doesn't? What gives you energy? Rather than follow the well-worn path, use what you know about your own strengths, embrace every challenge and make your journey as a professional unique to you."

We asked Iris: "What does a high performer look like to you?" She had this to say: "Someone who has an intrinsic drive to always do great, regardless of the activity. In truth, it is impossible to be great at everything, however having that drive will motivate you to always start with fresh eyes and give it your best shot."

———

With introductions made, it's time to unlock the first cipher ...

CHAPTER TWO

FULFILMENT

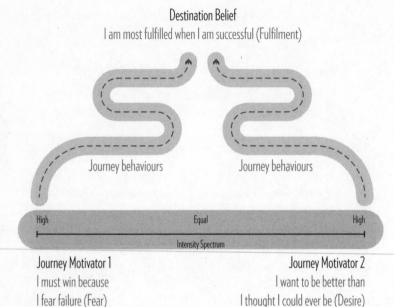

Destination Belief
I am most fulfilled when I am successful (Fulfilment)

Journey behaviours   Journey behaviours

High   Equal   High

Intensity Spectrum

Journey Motivator 1   Journey Motivator 2
I must win because   I want to be better than
I fear failure (Fear)   I thought I could ever be (Desire)

By interviewing high-performing salespeople for 90 minutes and exploring their individual motivations, we observed that they all had a burning desire to be successful, and a belief that success aids progression to both professional and personal fulfilment. No surprises there.

To ensure the study was reliable, we split participants into two groups. Group 1 included the highest-performing sellers in each participating company, and Group 2 included the lower performers.

Across both groups, we uncovered the Destination Belief that everyone held in common. When we explored what shaped that belief we uncovered two very different Journey Motivators.

That Destination Belief is: "I am most fulfilled when I am successful" (Fulfilment).

Journey Motivator 1 for Fulfilment is cautionary, motivated by fear, and focused on evading a negative consequence. ("I must win because I fear failure.")

Journey Motivator 2 for Fulfilment is aspirational. This is motivated by desire, and focused on seeking out a manageable level of risk to achieve change and open doors to new opportunity. ("I want to be better than I thought I could ever be.")

The Journey Motivators may sound like opposites – and they are – yet each plays its own role in achieving Fulfilment. We wondered if one was more effective than the other. Our research shows that while salespeople exhibit both Journey Motivators, they exhibit different levels of intensity, depending upon whether they are top- or low-performing. For example, 100% of high-performing salespeople are driven by Journey Motivator 2 (Desire) more intensely than Journey Motivator 1 (Fear).

For them, it turns out the carrot *is* more powerful than the stick.

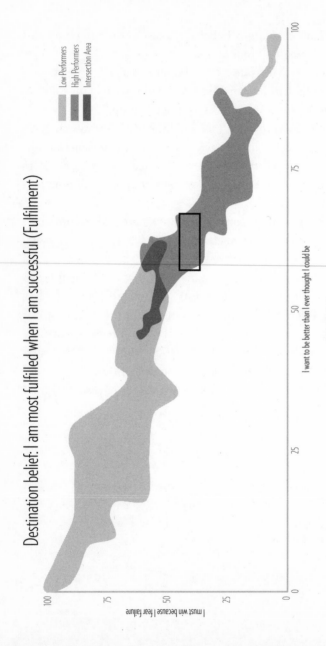

Destination belief: I am most fulfilled when I am successful (Fulfilment)

FIGURE 2

JOURNEY MOTIVATORS DISTRIBUTION FOR FULFILMENT

In *Figure 4*, the vertical axis reflects Journey Motivator 1 (Fear) and the horizontal axis shows Journey Motivator 2 (Desire). On its own, the graph looks like an ordinary scatter plot. But one piece of information is most exciting. Note the location of the rectangle. Our research found that the optimum position for the Fulfilment Destination Belief is 62% Desire and 38% Fear. The position of this tight cluster confirms that top salespeople hold both Journey Motivators, but the desire of the top 5% of high performers to be their best is nearly twice as strong as their fear of failure. This cluster of salespeople all have other things in common: they consistently rank in the top 5 percent of high performers. They sell more than anyone else. They earn more than their industry sector colleagues. Just to be clear as to how we arrived at this top 5%: from our high-performing group, we used a scorecard and ranked people north and south of a median. Then we isolated the top 5%, thus identifying the top 5% of the high-performing group. Let's back up a little and explain why we did this. We used a scorecard to create a level playing field and compare salespeople across x. For example, a quantitative measure such as 'Did this salesperson sell $1 million of business?' would not create a comparator because someone else could be a top performer selling $0.5 million of business. The people on our scorecard consistently hit targets for the last three years. Have they exceeded new customer acquisition over a certain period of time?

The belief system of the top 5% is fiercely pragmatic. They tap into fear like it's rocket fuel. It fires them up each morning, ignites their hunger and launches them into the thick of any opportunity they can find. But they're not perfectionists. They accept their limits and regard themselves as a 'continual work in progress,' where experimenting, failing, learning and improving are part of a refining process they embrace. It's a very similar mind-set to the Japanese concept of *kaizen*, where nothing is ever so good that it can't be continually improved.

With empirical evidence that the top 5% of sellers have this in common, understanding how you can adopt the same belief system is what we'll now explore.

JOURNEY MOTIVATOR 1:
'I MUST WIN BECAUSE I FEAR FAILURE.'

Atychiphobia is a word that originates from ancient Greek. *Atyches* means *unfortunate* and *phobos* means *fear*. It is the emotion that compels you to push your limits and endure discomfort because of a negative consequence if you don't. This drives everyday people to hit the gym in a quest to overcome physical weakness, loneliness or self-loathing. It drives them to study for a better professional qualification to avoid being passed over for promotion or getting stuck in a dead-end job. It drives salespeople to hit the streets early, make more calls, and be bold when closing business because they don't want to be seen as average, get crushed by debt, see their child denied the best education, or have an ageing parent without the best care.

This emotion is not about what good you gain, but what bad you avoid. It is sometimes called a "burning platform".

This phrase came out of the disastrous July 1988 explosion of the *Piper Alpha* oil-drilling platform off the coast of Scotland. A total of 164 crew and two rescuers lost their lives in the worst catastrophe in the history of North Sea oil exploration. One man who survived was superintendent engineer Andy Mochan. His is an extreme case of "winning to avoid failure." In his case, failure meant death.

Late at night a pressurized natural gas leak "screamed like a banshee" through the rig,[2] waking Andy and alerting others that something was wrong. Seconds later an explosion ripped the rig in two, engulfing it in a cloud of flame and acrid smoke. Andy groped in the dark to pull himself through a tangle of buckled corridors and reach the quaking platform above, where ignited oil rained down like napalm, melting the equipment, cabins and people it landed on. Andy briefly found a clear section of deck and hoped to stay in position until rescuers arrived. The rig had lifeboats, but they'd been incinerated. It had a helicopter pad, but this had collapsed. Backing away from an advancing wall of flame, Andy calculated what might happen if he were forced to jump the 15 storeys to the sea below.

If the fall didn't kill him, *if* he wasn't knocked senseless, *if* he wasn't impaled on floating debris, *if* he didn't shatter his arms and legs, *if* no heavy equipment fell on him, and *if* he avoided the globs of molten steel that rained down, *then* the frigid waters would certainly claim him. His training told him he'd have 20 minutes before he inevitably froze and drowned.

An explosion then sent a wall of flame hurtling toward him, and he had to decide: jump now or fry. Andy took one action to avoid a worse one. This was his *burning platform* moment. He jumped. Imagine what it might be like hurtling towards an ocean so cold that it would kill within minutes of immersion. The ice-cold ocean radiating ferocious heat from the oily flames on its surface, which were leaping into the air like fingers from hell, reaching up to pull Andy down to his fate.

Andy was burned severely, but was rescued and survived. Although his life was never the same again, he went on to lead a happy family life until his death in 2004. He also campaigned tirelessly on safety issues in the ensuing years. He never sought the changes in his personal world caused by the events on *Piper Alpha* that night, but he did ensure that lessons were learned and that something positive came out of a disaster which affected so many people.

Perhaps you're staring down a burning platform of your own, or may be required to face a major change in the future. How will you respond?

Andy jumped the 150 feet (45 meters) into the water. Looking back, he saw that the entire platform was ablaze – there was not a square foot of it that was not engulfed. Asked whether fear or desire motivates them more often, 100% of salespeople reveal that fear is a driver of behaviour to some extent, but the intensity levels for this differ between top- and low-performing salespeople.

We learned this by interviewing participants using semi-structured questions. These were established by our in-house psychologists, based on the theories of William Moulton Marston, inventor of the first lie-detector test, who published his findings in *Emotions of Normal People* in 1928.[3]

After these interviews, we separated respondents into two groups: those who held this Journey Motivator and those who did not. We analysed the first group for commonalities and identified ten behaviour traits held by all respondents.

Next, we triangulated these traits with the interview transcripts to confirm whether the scores were an accurate reflection of behaviour in each case. In short, we compared the language, examples used and behaviours referenced by the respondents with the questions posed by our psychometricians. This filtered out five behaviour traits that were not consistent, and revealed five traits that were consistent across each interview transcript. These findings are illustrated below.

Most frequently observed behaviours
1. Decisive / Unwavering
2. Self-starter / Independent
3. Commanding / Irresistible
4. Obstinate / Firm
5. Competitive / Winning mind-set

We learned that fear drives the majority (56%) of low-performing salespeople. Of those, 86% confess they are trying to avoid repeating the past. The two most common ways this was expressed in the research are: "I want more status or money than my family had growing up" or "I want to outperform a parent or rival's achievements." (This second conviction was sometimes expressed as, "I don't want to end up like my parents.")

One might think that, given this group's fear of failing, the behaviours highlighted in the table above would work to their advantage. If this is so, why then are they not top performers? It seems that in the ardent desire to avoid failure these behaviours may be over-extended, becoming counter-productive. It is what economists call the Law of Diminishing Returns. Unwavering becomes obdurate; independent becomes lone-wolf; commanding may become overbearing.

When asked, "What is ultimate success and fulfilment like, for you?" it was noteworthy that most low-performers could not describe what future state they wanted. Most had not taken the time to look ahead, envisage it or set new goals. They could describe in obsessive detail the conditions they were running from, but not what ideal they were running towards.

Can you see the problem with this? It's like driving a car by looking in the rear-view mirror. That which we think about most often shapes our belief system and attitudes. Our attitudes shape our character. Our character shapes our actions. Our actions shape what we achieve. Another way of saying this: "Attitude determines altitude."

If you spend most of your time poring over the past, you may be doomed to relive that past, not break away from it. There are several thoughts that English philosopher James Allen (1864–1912) wrote in the timeless *As a Man Thinketh*[4] that may apply:

- The soul attracts that … which it loves, and also that which it fears.
- Every action and feeling is preceded by a thought.
- Right thinking begins with the words we say to ourselves.
- You cannot travel within and stand still without.

A folk tale told by the Cherokee[5] might also be adapted here. A grandfather tells his grandson there are two wolves inside each person, which are always fighting. One of them is a good wolf that represents the future you want to arrive at. The other is a bad wolf that represents the past you fear repeating. The grandson looks up at his grandfather and says, "Which one will win?" The grandfather quietly replies, "The one you feed."

So, we see that fear of repeating a negative past drives most lower-performing salespeople. They may believe that remembering how bad the past was can have the effect of pumping them up to chase a better future. But the truth is that if you keep the past alive, you can never truly outgrow it. This is a flaw that potentially prevents low-performers from achieving the breakthroughs they need. If you've ever heard yourself or someone else utter, "That's just how it goes," "That's my lot in life," "There's nothing you can do about it," then you've been listening to the drumbeat of mediocrity.

Performance strategist Matt Mayberry says: "All top performers, regardless of profession, know the importance of picturing themselves succeeding in their minds before they actually do in reality. Consider these three examples. Boxing legend Muhammad Ali was always stressing the importance of seeing himself victorious long before the actual fight. As a struggling young actor, Jim Carrey used to picture himself being the greatest actor in the world. Basketball pro Michael Jordan always took the shot in his mind before he ever took one in real life. These top performers, among many others, mastered the technique of positive visualization and openly credit it as a success tactic. The truth is, if you can't picture yourself achieving a goal, chances are you won't. The more vivid you can get, the better it will work for you."[6]

We see that low-performing salespeople don't give themselves permission to make that leap, but rather stay anchored to a past that may be painful, disappointing, or parochial... but at least it's familiar. They've learned to cope. Secretly they might even enjoy complaining about how hard it is to get out of their current life. There are always ears willing to listen to, amplify and echo back the songs of mediocrity. These people claim to want better and are comforted in the hope that maybe one day their ship will come in. But, in reality, they have *settled* and are destined to eat, sleep, work and repeat. They may never reach true Fulfilment. They may always feel dissatisfied. The prize lies beyond their grasp because they're looking in the wrong direction. They're facing the past, not the future.

We also noted in the research process that many low-performing salespeople are practised in the art of self-deception. At face value, they told us their Journey Motivator is an intense fear of failure. Yet we recognized a pattern of linguistics in the interview transcripts that revealed "fear of failure" is actually a deflection from a deeper truth. Many low-performing salespeople, it seems, may be afraid of accountability.

Let's back up and explain this. Failure is a faceless concept with no identity. As such, people prefer to see it as a thing that happens to them outside their control, rather than it being a manifestation of their own attitudes, actions or inaction. It's a submission to the fates, to the planets, to the daily horoscope – a habit of being acted upon rather than taking action. Not believing one is in charge of the outcome becomes an excuse for failure.

In a moment of raw honesty, one salesperson commented how awful it can be to face failure with a gnawing sense of accountability: "If I am unsuccessful, I am the failure. No thanks!" Deep down there's a prevailing sense that any failure is negative, a source of shame, ridicule and comparison, or defines a person as being broken or of low worth. In this group, we saw virtually no recognition that failure could be viewed as a positive reference point to learn from. Rather, the consensus was that it should be avoided at all costs. And most were at pains to point out to us that this belief was a virtue. They wore this badge with pride.

Where does this attitude come from? It's different for everyone. Perhaps as children they had strict, demanding parents and resolved never to be pushed around as an adult. Maybe they were never held accountable for completing chores and grew to adulthood never learning to try, fail, own up and step up. Some who are raised in a drive-through, on-demand, click-and-deliver world may enjoy eating the harvest but know nothing about earning it through trial and error. Those whose first taste of corporate life was a culture of pressurized perfection may be horrified by the thought of any mistake that could cause a loss of face or fall from grace.

For these people, failure is something they run from, it is not a familiar companion, and as such its value as a teacher is not understood. So, they stick to what they know, cover their butt, check everything twice, and when failure inevitably arrives, some go to pieces. Others start polishing their CV or résumé. Some might even massage their numbers, gloss over their errors, or point a finger at someone else. It's self-imploding in the long-term, and others can get caught in the blast zone.

Now let's work some numbers. If you work in a sales force of 100 people, by the law of averages 50 will be higher performers and 50 will be lower performers. We discovered earlier that fear drives some 56% of low-performers, and 86% of them have a specific fear of repeating past failures, so they dodge, deflect or deceive to avoid a repeat performance. Based on this, a sales force of 100 people will statistically have 24 people holding on to this belief system. That's essentially 25% of our sales population being driven to behave in this way by dark, self-defeating beliefs.

A fear-averse attitude kills creativity and atrophies the muscles needed to push boundaries. Think for a moment what type of salesperson this creates. Will they cold-call, go prospecting, follow up on leads, attempt a trial close or ask for the order? Will they be more likely or less likely to research their customers and take the gamble that they've interpreted their needs well enough to engage in a credible whiteboard session or verbal discussion? Or, are they more likely to give a safe, pre-prepared pitch from a slide deck or brochure?

Does your HR function weed out people with self-limiting beliefs during the recruitment process? There are screening procedures designed to do so. We know from the research that a sales force will sell more when staffed by people motivated by desire more than fear. In an ideal world, this would be a data point when selecting new recruits. But for the myriad salespeople already employed, the good news is that this self-limiting belief can be re-programmed. Nobody need stay a prisoner of their past belief system.

As Denis E. Waitley, an American motivational speaker, once wrote: "The simple truth is no success was ever achieved without failure. Failure should be our teacher, not our undertaker. Failure is delay, not defeat. It is a temporary detour, not a dead end. Failure is something we can avoid only by saying nothing, doing nothing, and being nothing."[7]

Thomas Edison made 10,000 attempts to create the light bulb. His attitude was, "I have not failed 10,000 times. I have not failed once. I have succeeded in proving that those 10,000 ways will not work."[8] James Dyson took 5,127 attempts to invent the dual cyclone vacuum cleaner that eventually made him a billionaire.[9]

In the same way, 80% of sales require five follow-up calls, yet 92% of salespeople give up on a prospect within four rejections and 44% abandon the pursuit after just one rejection![10] The rags-to-riches *Harry Potter* author J. K. Rowling also writes on this topic: "Failure is so important. We speak about success all the time. It is the ability to … use failure that often leads to greater success. I've met people who don't want to try for fear of failing."

So, failure is fine if it isn't used as an excuse for mediocrity. Each year presents 365 fresh starts. On any morning, the risk-averse, looking-backwards, afraid-of-accountability, low-performing salesperson can choose to face the future, own their actions, and *transform*.

The first step is to envision a new future that breaks free from old scripts.

In our research group, 78% of low-performers had no idea what they really wanted from their life and career in any specific or measurable terms. They weren't goal-setters.

The opportunity here is not to ignore the fear of failure, but to control it and channel your energy to define and reach a new destination. By doing so, you will reduce the intensity of fear and uncertainty and replace it with the desire to achieve that new horizon and become better than you ever thought you could be.

JOURNEY MOTIVATOR 2: 'I WANT TO BE BETTER THAN I THOUGHT I COULD EVER BE.'

Results are important in the sales profession. Everyone has the same goal: move leads through various gates until the buyer exchanges cash for goods or services. But some salespeople perform better than others. What makes the difference?

High-performers hold a different intensity of Journey Motivator from low-performers. They have a destination in mind. They give themselves permission to rise above the herd and become better than was previously thought possible by them, by others, or by what past experience suggested they were capable of. They believe that success in its various forms brings fulfilment, and therefore greater success brings greater fulfilment.

One of our 'iconics', Louis Jordan, sums this mind-set up perfectly when he talks about failure. "I think there is always, for me, a fear of not achieving things because you have not been resourceful enough to work something out. A disappointment for me would be where, in retrospect, there was an opportunity to be successful, but you missed it. I will give you an example of where that would be implied. If you were under-prepared and didn't empathize with the people that you were pitching to, and then later realized that. That would be a disappointment. I would fear that happening. The failed mission to Mars, on the other hand, is not something I fear. Allow yourself to have coaching right from the beginning. Coaching is a strength, not a weakness. Find out what you need to know and then know it. Do it at the fastest rate you can."

Note how Louis frames the prospect of failure as disappointment with himself for not being the best he could possibly be. We are what we repeatedly do. Excellence is not an act, but a ritual we habitually practise in ways small and large. Day by day, inch by inch, you can move any aspect of your life and make it better. Experiment on this by answering this question:

By the time I go to sleep tonight, how will I be a better version of me than when I woke this morning?

Low-performers feel threatened by this question because it implies change is possible and personal accountability is required. Yet it's a question top performers ask themselves daily.

They start by examining the different roles they play in life, and the different actions required in each role. For example, you might play the roles of salesperson, father, son and friend. Or you might be manager, daughter, sister and volunteer. Each role is an aspect of your multifaceted life, and each one needs to be managed and balanced in order for you to feel centred and fulfilled.

Have you ever written each role you play as a heading on separate pages in a notebook? How about taking some time out each day to write goals for each role? If you don't do this already, it's simple to begin, right now, today. Find a quiet space where you can really think. Turn off your electronic devices. Use the time to jot down what's truly important to you in each different aspect of your life, and lay plans to achieve these goals. Then, as you achieve them, write new ones, and keep moving forward. Giving yourself permission to spend as little as ten minutes a day to perform this ritual can make a huge difference. Doing so will be the start of a powerful new habit. What you think about most often, you become.

We found that 88% of low-performers demonstrated a belief in their interview responses that other people were better, luckier, more privileged, born in the right place, or get all the breaks. It's called Inferiority Complex and is described by our in-house psychologists as an unrealistic feeling of general inadequacy caused by actual or supposed inferiority in one sphere. This may manifest itself in the form of overtly hostile or passive-aggressive behaviour towards others.

This negative mantra paints success as something only other people can enjoy. It's self-limiting. This is a belief system that top-performers shatter, for as psychologist and author Henry C. Link (1889–1952) comments, "While one person hesitates because he feels inferior, another is busy making mistakes and becoming superior."

The successful salespeople we spoke to all wanted to be better than they once thought possible. To achieve this, brutal honesty was required. They had to get real with themselves. One said: "It can bruise your ego to admit you're not as good as you want to be. But you must take the jackhammer to your current life and break things up. This invariably involves personal sacrifice. You have to exchange the beliefs and behaviours that hold you back for new ones that move you toward fulfilment."

Our iconic salesperson Justin Stone, of J. P. Morgan, told us what fulfilment means to him: "Early in my career I just wanted the next commission cheque, the next holiday, my own house. As I achieved these, my definition of fulfilment changed. Now that I have a wife and child and more security, I think about the legacy I'll leave to others. What made me happy in my thirties isn't what gets me up in the mornings now. To gain clarity I hired a great coach. I wish I'd done this much earlier. It's healthy to do a personal diagnostic, check the brakes, change the oil and reset the satellite navigation, like you do with a car."

Justin's story may resonate with you. What made him happy at a younger age no longer satisfied him later in life because he'd achieved his original goals. And so, while sustaining these, he added new ones. His capacity to achieve had increased. The canvas he was painting on had expanded.

Yet despite his success, Justin remained grounded by holding on to a moderate fear of failure. Yes, even high-performers fear failure, but unlike the low-performers it isn't their dominant paradigm. They *balance* fear of failure with the desire to excel. Without this balance, people feel they are bulletproof, with nothing to lose or nothing to prove. This can lead to arrogant, reckless or self-absorbed behaviour.

In fact, the *very bottom* 5% of low-performers don't act like low-performers at all, but as an extreme version of high-performers. Like wolves of Wall Street, these sellers exhibit huge appetite and desire, but feel zero fear. This is where too much of a good thing goes wrong. Their behaviour creates compromises and gaps that can only be papered over for so long before the house of cards collapses. Our findings are consistent with *The Harvard Business Review*, which classifies these types of executives as "Surgeons." Research published by Hill, Mellon, Laker and Goddard (2016) concluded that "Surgeons are both decisive and incisive … they've always enjoyed winning and strongly believe that you win if you're fit, train hard and have the right attitude." But they break rules, take risks and sense no boundaries; they are a law unto themselves. They only focus on the here and now, and don't have time to look at anything else. They may talk a good game, but cause more problems than they solve.[11]

Louis Jordan's perspective on fulfilment and success is illuminating. "I find the concept of fulfilment quite difficult because it is a bit like island-hopping in the Caribbean. Just when you think you have found the greatest sea with the best snorkelling and the most shaded palm trees, you realize that the next island might be slightly better. So, while you might be happy on island A there is always a draw to island B. The difference between success and fulfilment is that island A is success, but island B is the anticipation of what is next. Perhaps fulfilment is something that is just at the end of your fingertips."

"I had no grand plan when I left university, but there was an ambition with aims in it," he said. "It was to have the maximum amount of ability to choose. My aim was to be part of something I enjoyed and was good at. That had to involve creating something and being part of something worthy. It also had to be something that had integrity; something I wouldn't be scared to stand behind."

"I can't think of a time when I didn't think like that. Growing up in the North-East [of England] I saw people without options losing their jobs; and when they lost their jobs they lost their income and choices. That probably made me think there is a better design to life, to success and fulfilment. I have always seen money as a utensil to achieve things, but in itself I don't think there is any excitement to be gained from looking at bank statements."

It seems that the key to success is moderation: just enough desire, and just enough fear. That's how high-performers fly. Like a rocket on the launchpad, if you don't apply enough thrust, gravity will keep you on the ground. Even after lift-off, if you don't apply enough thrust, gravity will bring you back down. There are always two opposing forces at play. In the case of Fulfilment, it's forward thrust (desire) versus gravity (fear).

When you calibrate these so that desire is stronger than fear, you gain higher altitude. You don't want to rush into orbit too quickly or the capsule might shake apart. You don't want to rise too slowly or you won't achieve escape velocity. Astronauts keep the rocket's ascent balanced with just the right trajectory and velocity to rise above the world.

In our research, we looked at the behaviour traits consistent across each interview transcript and the corresponding behaviour analysis profile for this group. Here's what we found:

Most frequently observed behaviours
1. Enthusiastic / Optimistic
2. Fun-loving / Humorous
3. Sense of adventure / Thrill of the unknown
4. Energetic / Thriving
5. Competitive / Winning mind-set

Salespeople driven by the Journey Motivator of desire accept failure *and* appreciate that their career includes ups and downs, peaks and valleys. Publilius Syrus, the ancient Latin writer of moral maxims, said, "It is foolish to fear what you cannot avoid." Those who embody the Journey Motivator regard achievement as taking pleasure in surprising themselves, in proving to themselves and others that they have gone further than anyone thought possible.

Iconic salesperson Dilip Mailvaganam, of Microsoft, told us, "Most of my background is in start-ups and that is my real passion. Everything is down to you. It is a lot of small companies within a large organization. I have tended to want to own things myself, but it is important to let others help, in terms of a global team. The whole culture of Microsoft is starting to change because they, like me, believe life is about failing in order to learn."

Dilip's description of Microsoft's culture in his division is indicative of a high-performing sales team. People on this team accept that failure is inevitable, so continuously look ahead and don't rest on their laurels. Being better than they ever thought possible is a life passion.

We identified passion in every salesperson who sought the goal of fulfilment through the Journey Motivator of being better than they ever thought possible. Their passion was not always work-related. Top sellers have private passions too.

Tom Cunliffe, COO of Toshiba, is an accomplished cyclist. Phil Benton, sales director at Adidas, is a talented hockey player. Erica Feidner, whom Inc. magazine dubbed "one of the ten greatest salespeople of all time" in 2011, is a world-class pianist.

Not every passion is in the public eye. Some high-performers are green-fingered gardeners, prolific genealogists, loyal volunteers or avid readers.

What is passion, and how is it different from a passing interest? A passion is something you can't live without. When it's missing from your life you feel a hole that gnaws at you. You constantly wish that you were doing, living, being or having it. If you've read the book *Talk Like TED*[12] you will be familiar with the question, "What makes your heart sing?" We use this question when coaching and we receive amazing answers!

Passion is what gets high-performers out of their beds every morning. Fear gets the low-performers out of bed every morning. Consider how it feels to wake up with passion, with your heart singing. Now consider how it feels to wake up with fear. What drives you makes a difference in your performance.

We are not saying your passion must be exclusively related to selling. In fact, none of the iconic salespeople we interviewed declared sales as their personal passion. But they were all passionate about *something*. The ability to feel and commit deeply was in their emotional make-up and this makes a substantial difference in how they throw themselves at life and at their career.

You may be asking yourself if it is true that *only* top performers displayed a passion for something. The fact is that around 10% of low performers declared that they had a passion. However, it seems that the passion was used almost as a form of escape, rather than something that created positive energy that was then channelled into professional success. In the end, it comes down to our choice. We can choose to escape from our sales role, or we can choose to channel our passion towards achieving that "escape velocity." These are obviously two very different outcomes. When you focus on the things you are passionate about you're more likely to seek to recreate them in your wider life. The feeling's good, so why not be better than you ever thought you could be?

———

On the next pages are some thought-provokers about Fulfilment. Find a quiet place, contemplate the questions, and write down your responses. Doing so will start you on the journey of applying the Salesperson's Secret Code.

Following that, we have provided additional insights about Fulfilment, which were shared by the iconic salespeople we interviewed around the world for our research.

MY FULFILMENT REVIEW

Q1. What fear limits me and what impact does this have?

Q2. What breakthroughs would I like to achieve? What's stopping me?

Q3. What desires motivate me?

Q4. What is true success and fulfilment like for me?

Q5. For me to feel fulfilled, what has to happen?

ADDITIONAL FULFILMENT INSIGHTS FROM TOP-PERFORMING SALESPEOPLE

1. Decide what "makes your heart sing", what you are most passionate about, what gets you out of bed in the morning and keeps you working late. This defines your purpose.

2. Choose what "personal brand" you want people to use when they describe you to others. Jeff Bezos, founder and CEO of Amazon, said: "Your brand is what people say about you when you're not in the room."

3. Turn adversity into a positive, whether it's an economic downturn, competitive threat, shrinking market or office politics. "Chasing a good opportunity" causes you to behave differently than when you're "avoiding a bad consequence." See your cup as half full, not half empty.

4. Give yourself a chance to stand out from the crowd. Study, educate yourself, acquire new knowledge and skills. The fact that you are reading this book shows that you are a curious person. Revel in that curiosity; show that you respect yourself.

5. Identify an aspirational role model. If they're in your personal network, arrange to meet, and ask how they overcome fear and limiting beliefs. If they're outside your personal network, follow their blogs, articles and news feeds.

6. If you are in strategic sales that can take a long time to close, set some short-term goals so you can celebrate short-term attainment on the path to the big win. This keeps motivation levels high.

7. Beyond your business targets, set private goals each week and reward yourself for achieving them.

WHAT'S IN THE MIND?

The psychologist says...

Fulfilment is not a new concept in the world of social sciences. In fact, in the 1950s American psychologist Abraham Maslow studied the human *hierarchy of needs* and what motivates us to do what we do each day. Maslow found that a need influences a person's activities until it has been satisfied. There are five fundamental human needs, and as each one is satisfied it ceases to motivate. The most basic needs (such as food, shelter, warmth, security) must be satisfied first before higher ones can motivate. The highest need Maslow's theory identifies is self-actualization, also known as self-fulfilment.

Self-fulfilment refers to the need for personal growth and discovery that is present throughout an individual's life. For a salesperson, this can drive their desire to be the best-of-the-best and to achieve personal goals and business targets. In doing so, they are fulfilling their own needs and, in turn, realizing their capabilities. It is important to spend some time uncovering what truly motivates you as an individual to work toward fulfilment. This helps to counterbalance the inevitable feelings of uncertainty and fear of failure which all of us face from time to time. It's rare that you meet anyone who wakes up in the morning and says to themselves, "Today I am going to be rubbish at what I do!" Human beings want to succeed. The trick is to ensure the positive self-actualizing mind-set more often than the negative and inhibiting one. What do you feel most passionate about? Why do you do what you do? Used correctly, this is powerful insight for sales managers and leaders.

Motivational techniques can be used to focus on helping each salesperson feel fulfilled. These range from the obvious monetary reward, to new learning opportunities, personal recognition, to having a sense of belonging in a wider, successful team, etc. Understanding each person's journey towards self-actualization helps managers and salespeople focus motivation most effectively and increases the likelihood that both parties will be satisfied by the achievement of their commercial and personal ambitions, targets and goals.

THE LAST WORD ON FULFILMENT

The Elephant and the Rope

In beautiful, verdant Sri Lanka, high up in the mountains on the road to Kandy, is an elephant orphanage. The animals are well cared for and treated with kindness and respect. The visitors, upon whom the orphanage depends for most of its income, are encouraged to come into a clearing in the forest to touch and stroke the magnificent creatures. Up close and personal the elephants look incredibly wise. The more observant visitor might notice that each elephant has a small rope tied loosely around one ankle. The elephants can break away at any moment because the rope has no strength. The reason for this is that when the elephants are young the keepers use the same rope and it is enough to hold them. When they grow to adulthood they still believe that the rope can hold them, so they never attempt to break free.

How many of us are just like the elephants of Sri Lanka?

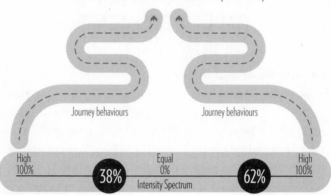

Destination Belief
I am most fulfilled when I am successful (Fulfilment)

Journey behaviours   Journey behaviours

High
100%
Equal
0%
38%   62%
Intensity Spectrum
High
100%

Journey Motivator 1
I must win because
I fear failure (Fear)

Journey Motivator 2
I want to be better than
I thought I could ever be (Desire)

100 percent of salespeople reveal fear is a driver to some extent, but its prevalence differs between top - and low-performing salespeople

100 percent of high-performing salespeople are driven by desire more intensely than fear. They are constantly evaluating themselves against a personal progress goal to be the most professional, productive salesperson they can be

Like a rocket on the launchpad, if you don't apply enough thrust, gravity will keep you on the ground. Even after lift-off, if you don't apply enough thrust, gravity will bring you back down. There are always two opposing forces at play. In the case of Fulfilment, it's forward thrust (desire) versus gravity (fear). When you arrange these so desire is stronger than fear, you gain a higher altitude. You don't want to rush into orbit too quickly or the capsule might shake apart. You don't want to rise too slowly or you won't achieve escape velocity. Astronauts keep the rocket's ascent balanced with just the right trajectory and velocity to rise above the world.

56 percent of low-performing salespeople are driven by fear of failure and 86 percent of these have a specific fear of repeating past failures. so they dodge. deflect or deceive to avoid them

78 percent of low-performers had no idea what they really want from their life and career in any specific or measurable term. They weren't goal-setters

The very bottom five percent of low-performers don't act like low-performers at all, but as an extreme version of high-performers. Like wolves of Wall Street. these sellers exhibit huge appetite and desire. but feel zero fear

CHAPTER THREE

CONTROL

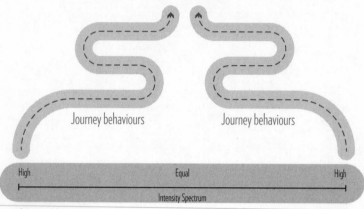

Destination Belief
Someone or something must always be accountable for success (Control)

Journey behaviours   Journey behaviours

High   Equal   High

Intensity Spectrum

Journey Motivator 1
There is only so much
I can control (Victim)

Journey Motivator 2
I am ultimately responsible
for my own destiny (Hero)

Salespeople understand the concept of *Control*, the Destination Belief of the code. They believe *someone or something must always be accountable for success,* and so they evaluate where they want to be in the future, where they are today, what gap they need to bridge, and what forces can help or hinder them in achieving their goals. The top-performers display strong personal accountability for success and failure, and seldom shift blame. Should failure come they don't blame the economy, weak sales leads or their pricing policy. They own the problem and learn from it, seeing failure as a temporary detour, not a destination – something to learn from and apply next time.

Across our two groups of salespeople, where in each participating company Group 1 included the highest-performing sellers and Group 2 held the lowest-performing, we uncovered two opposing Journey Motivators.

Journey Motivator 1 asserts that not every outcome can be guaranteed. It holds that *there is only so much I can control.* In part this echoes Helmuth von Moltke, the 19th-century Prussian army commander who pioneered new, more modern methods of directing troops in the field. To paraphrase von Moltke, "No battle plan ever survives first contact with the enemy."[13] Or, as the boxer Mike Tyson put it far more colourfully, "Everyone has a plan until they get punched in the mouth." When it comes to salespeople with a high intensity score on this Journey Motivator, however, this pragmatism is laced with reticence. They don't appear to throw their *all* at a venture. They hold back from full commitment because deep down they expect their efforts may go wrong, and want to reserve the right to tell themselves they didn't play the fool for believing too deeply. For sake of abbreviation, we call this Journey Motivator a *Victim* mentality. It shapes people's impression of how little Control they are likely to have over any situation, how hard they try to shape their destiny before giving up, and how easily they may allow others (like customers or sales managers) to take charge of a discussion.

Journey Motivator 2 for Control reveals full ownership and accountability for results. It reads: *I am ultimately responsible for my own destiny.* This is incredibly brave. As the father of modern psychology Sigmund Freud wrote: "Most people do not really want freedom, because freedom involves responsibility, and most people are frightened of responsibility."[14] Yet salespeople who hold this Journey Motivator see full ownership as the only real guarantee of gaining or maintaining control, and the freedom and rewards it brings. For the sake of abbreviation, we call this Journey Motivator a *Hero* mentality.

At first glance these Journey Motivators appear to be diametrically opposed: one puts you on the hook for outcomes, the other lets you off it. But there's more nuance in the way high-performers interpret them.

When high-performers hear the inner voice of Journey Motivator 1 telling them, *There is only so much I can control,* they start processing how much risk they're willing to tolerate, and form a mental checklist of the actions needed to mitigate that risk. They can't help it. This is an automatic 'can do' response as they prepare to jump in. Lower performers, however, approach it as though the cup were only half full, lowering their expectations for what's possible, and emotionally excusing themselves for below-par results… just in case.

These are clearly different levels of confidence in the outcome: one deciding to act *(Hero)*, the other allowing themselves to be acted upon *(Victim)*.

When high-performers hear the second Journey Motivator whispering, *I am ultimately responsible for my own destiny*, it's a liberating, energizing war cry to be more adventurous, courageous or opportunistic, to create the best destiny possible and take credit for the outcome. Conversely, low-performers hear the same whisper and interpret its intention very differently. They don't trust that inner voice, fearing they're being set up to be blamed for something. "Ultimately responsible" translates as *you won't be able to point the finger at someone else.* "Destiny" translates as *trapped.* High and low performers process this same Journey Motivator through an entirely different filter.

We explored the possibility of one Journey Motivator being more productive than the other. Our research shows that salespeople need both, but not in equal balance. Every high-performing salesperson held the Hero Journey Motivator more intensely than the Victim Journey Motivator.

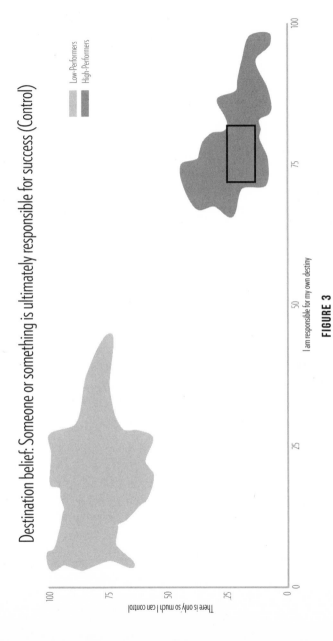

Destination belief: Someone or something is ultimately responsible for success (Control)

FIGURE 3

JOURNEY MOTIVATORS DISTRIBUTION FOR CONTROL

As shown on *Figure 3* our research concludes that the optimum position for the Control Destination Belief is 78% internal responsibility (the Hero acting on events, on the horizontal axis) and 22% external responsibility (the Victim being acted upon, on the vertical axis). This optimal positioning is indicated by the rectangle. The position of this tight cluster confirms that top salespeople hold both Journey Motivators, but the Hero Journey Motivator is three times more powerful than the Victim Journey Motivator in high-performers.

With empirical evidence that the top 5% of sellers have this in common, understanding how you can adopt the same belief system is what we'll now explore.

JOURNEY MOTIVATOR 1: 'THERE IS ONLY SO MUCH I CAN CONTROL.' (VICTIM)

Fifty percent of respondents believe they have a limited window of control over their sales, career, life or other people. They feel they know themselves well enough to see what they are good at and where they still struggle. They use this self-knowledge to live their life colouring inside the lines, where it's safe, familiar and manageable.

Salespeople who hold this Journey Motivator to a high intensity feel powerful – even lucky – in a familiar territory, yet often powerless on new turf. Tennis, squash and basketball players refer to a "home court advantage" when they're playing at a location they know and are comfortable with. The Chinese culture devotes significant attention to the concept of Feng Shui, where location affects a person's flow of energy, which in turn affects how well they perform and succeed in their personal and professional life.[15] Whether you believe in invisible energy or not, we certainly heard account managers explain how being assigned to a new location placed them at a disadvantage, changed their energy and stripped away their control, so the inevitable failure was not their fault. "When I'm on the right type of account I am excellent," they said. "But now that I've been moved to *the wrong account*, I can't hit my target."

The words "wrong" and "can't" reveal a fixed mind-set, where failure is a *fait accompli*. If circumstances don't line up exactly as they want, some victims believe they have lost control and can't win it back. They throw their hands in the air, pack up their toys and go home. But as the saying goes, misery loves company. So, it is common for these victims to confess their frustrations of hopelessness to colleagues, lacing their tales of woe with just enough authenticity that others may begin to question if they are affected by the same so-called "deficiencies" in the company's systems, procedures or management techniques. This is how worms in one bad apple can spoil an entire barrel.

Former USAF pilot and New York Times bestselling author of *Illusions*, *The Bridge Across Forever* and *Jonathan Livingstone Seagull*, Richard Bach, once observed: "If it's never our fault, we can't take responsibility for it. If we can't take responsibility for it, we'll always be its victim."[16] Avoiding responsibility for our actions encourages mediocrity. It stunts growth, both personal and professional.

Have you ever heard a salesperson who missed their target say: "My quota is too high," "The pricing strategy is wrong," "The leads are weak" or, "The product is too old?" Are they accepting responsibility for outcomes, or being a victim?

What about the last time *you* lost a potential sale? Can you pinpoint the exact moment it slipped away? Was it outside your control as a victim of circumstance, or might improved planning, stronger preparation, greater curiosity, a higher call rate, more listening, improved assertiveness or faster follow-through have earned you that commission?

When exploring this Journey Motivator, what surprised our researchers is that most low-performers don't even know they are low-performers. They consider themselves among the most enlightened of people; brave, courageous, optimistic, industrious souls, denied greatness only by other people's mistakes or an unfavourable twist of fate.

Such was the case for would-be bank robber McArthur Wheeler, who held up two banks in Pittsburgh in 1995.[17] He believed he had a foolproof disguise by painting his face with lemon juice, knowing this was a key ingredient in invisible ink. As long as he didn't pass under an ultraviolet light or walk too close to a heat source, he was convinced the bank's security cameras wouldn't capture his image. Wheeler was genuinely perplexed when police arrested him within hours of the crime.

Charles Darwin noted in 1871: "Ignorance more frequently begets confidence than does knowledge."[18] So it was Wheeler's absolute certainty of success in defiance of all known physical laws that inspired psychologists David Dunning of Cornell University and Justin Kruger of New York University's Stern School of Business to study this type of mind-set. They noted that when people are incompetent they suffer a dual burden: not only do they reach false conclusions and make poor choices, but their incompetence robs them of the ability to see themselves as they really are, and hence denies them a needed wake-up call.

Dunning and Kruger's research was published in 1999 in the *Journal of Personality and Social Psychology* headlined, "Unskilled and Unaware of It: How Difficulties in Recognizing One's Own Incompetence Lead to Inflated Self-Assessments."[19] In 2005 *Harvard Business Review* wrote an article on the study, snappily titled: "Those Who Can't, Don't Know It."[20] The conclusions show that incompetent people don't achieve most standards set for them, find excuses for their own incompetence, and don't recognize higher competence in others. They go through life stubbornly oblivious to their actual state.

Across four separate studies, Dunning and Kruger's test subjects grossly overestimated their abilities: in tests for grammar, logic and humour they scored low in the 12th percentile, yet they guessed they were up in the 62nd. This miscalibration was linked to deficits in metacognitive skill, or the capacity to distinguish accuracy from error. Hence, failure was never their fault – it was the world stacking the deck against them. This is the psychological basis to the Victim Journey Motivator.

The behaviour traits that were consistent across each interview transcript, and the corresponding behavioural model profile for people holding the Victim Journey Motivator for Control, are listed below.

Most frequently observed behaviours
1. Eager / Impatient
2. Aggressive
3. Forceful character / Powerful
4. Optimistic
5. Daring / Gutsy

Our in-house psychologists found that these people are decisive, task-oriented individuals with high optimism and personality. This doesn't sound like a victim who under-performs at all! This is one reason why discovering The Salesperson's Secret Code is so important. On their own, personality assessments and psychometric tests provide a fantastic framework for understanding broad behavioural types, but they don't reveal all the underlying beliefs.

For example, picture a salesperson who appears driven, influential and likely to climb any mountain. But imagine if, during that ascent, a storm of difficulty blows up the mountain-face. Perhaps it's a setback or loss in their personal life. Rain and hail sting their face and, disoriented, they lose sight of the summit. At the same time a guide rope – one of their commercial tethers – snaps from its carabiner and sends them falling backwards towards a cliff. Perhaps they were passed over for promotion, or lost a key account. Now they're in freefall, out of control – a victim of circumstance. Just before sliding off the mountain altogether, they find a hand-sized crevice, stab their fingers into it and pull to an abrupt stop mere feet from the edge. Heart pounding, wind howling, they move to stand – and as the ground slides several inches they recognise the bluff is covered by a bed of loose shale. The more they move, the more it slides. Now they're convinced the slightest movement will take them over the edge. So, they hold their breath and lie very still.

Experience causes some people to believe the *status quo ante* (the way things are) is safer than the *status mutatio* (a change of state), or that their current state is as good as it's ever going to get. They settle in where they are, desperate not to slide backwards, but too timid to climb upwards. Such a belief system doesn't always show up in behavioural preference psychometrics. The Destination Beliefs and Journey Motivators uncovered in The Salesperson's Secret Code underscore the message that as we believe, so we will most likely behave.

Beliefs shape awareness, which moulds ambition, which colours motivation, which sculpts attitude, which affects behaviour, which encourages learning, which informs skill, which drives actions, which determine results.

Let's liken a salesperson's performance to the body of a racing car. We see the shape, the style and colour, assembled and ready to hit the road. A person's education and skills might be likened to fuel in the tank; the more they have, the farther they'll go. Their needs, ambition and hunger might be likened to spark plugs that ignite the fuel to create combustion to drive the wheels. Within this analogy, where do a person's belief systems fit in? They're at the driver's feet: the accelerator and brake. It doesn't matter how suited to a selling role a psychometric assessment says a person is if deeply held beliefs make them drive with the brakes on.

You can, therefore, profile a salesperson against all reasonable indicators and conclude they should be successful. They have a winning psychometric profile. They attended all the right training courses. They have a clever customer relationship management package with auto alerts and social marketing. They're blessed with a steady stream of incoming sales-ready leads. Their sales manager conscientiously gives them three hours of skills coaching each month. Their team contributes meaningfully to opportunity reviews designed to help them win the biggest deals in their pipeline. Their commission plan and other rewards are motivational. The seller will act and talk as expected, and be seen doing many of the things expected of a top sales professional. Yet, deep down, they'll hold back. Despite every system and support, you can still fail if your inner monologue taunts, "There is only so much I can control."

In the previous chapter on Fulfilment you'll recall that we explored the Journey Motivators of Desire and Fear. We looked for connective tissue between each segment of code, examining the extent to which the Control Journey Motivators of Victim and Hero in this chapter match those for Fulfilment in the previous chapter. Not too surprisingly we found a 100% match between salespeople who hold the Fear Journey Motivator and those who hold the Victim Journey Motivator.

What do low-performers fear most? Anything that shatters the cognitive illusion that they're actually a high-performer who is only disadvantaged by circumstance. To face the truth about themselves would be too confronting, too crushing, too cruel. This doesn't only reveal itself in business, according to sales effectiveness expert Nic Read. "It's getting a bad grade at school, and blaming the teacher," he said. "It's losing a sports match, and blaming the equipment. It's having a bad day, and blaming the horoscope."

This defeatist attitude of victimization, so evident in low-performers, finds a cure in the second Journey Motivator, which we'll examine now.

JOURNEY MOTIVATOR 2: 'I AM ULTIMATELY RESPONSIBLE FOR MY OWN DESTINY.' (HERO)

In our interview questions, one key query was: "To improve your current success, what would you change?" The answers are revealing. The majority of low-performers replied using words that could be summarized as, "Not a lot. I'm great as I am." Most high-performers replied, "Everything! I make small course corrections every day." The high-performers' answer echoes something the philosopher Confucius wrote over two thousand years ago: "To know thyself is the beginning of wisdom."[21] He was talking about self-awareness and self-actualization.

Accordingly, 100% of high-performing salespeople hold the Hero Journey Motivator: "I am ultimately responsible for my own destiny' is markedly more intense when it comes to their approach to Control. When we cross-reference back to the earlier chapter on Fulfilment, 100% of these same salespeople also hold the Desire Journey Motivator, "I want to be better than I thought I could ever be."

The people in this group recognize that energy gets depleted as you climb the path of self-mastery, and needs to be replaced. They generate positive emotions like hope and resourcefulness through interacting positively with other people, and choosing to respond positively to the events around them. When we looked at the interview transcripts of this group we saw a pattern of behaviour that could be summarized in the following three points:

1. **Engaging** with what they want to control or master.
2. **Effecting** change in their circumstances and environment through actively influencing outcomes.
3. **Evolving** new mind-sets and behaviours to set themselves up for future success.

In essence, the high-performers seek to change the world and are prepared to be changed by the world.

Iris Schoenmakers told us she changed the world using a pair of pink high-heels. "Sometimes you find yourself in a situation where you have very little time to achieve the maximum effect. That happened to me when I was leading the Channel Change Management programme for Cisco. There was a major change effort underway which appeared to be progressing well, but the internal sales teams were resisting the changes I was seeking to implement to their part of the process. This would have had a major impact on the overall success of the project. I had built my reputation in the Channel, but this is a global business and most internal sales people would understandably not recognize me. The first time I presented to one of our sales teams they did not seem too eager to listen to this lady with a corporate role who was telling them what to do differently in their own job. As the project was in full flight and I needed to cover many countries in Europe, Africa and the Middle East, I could only stay a few days per country – not quite enough time to build trust and traction with the local sales teams. The solution? Not so obvious. To build a brand overnight that challenges stereotypes, translates across cultures and is unique enough to be linked to the expertise of one individual calls for some out-of-the-box thinking, which came to me during a shopping spree.

I love my shoes and I had the inspiration to turn this to my professional advantage", Iris said. "I bought the loudest pink shoes I could find. After that, each country I visited would experience the tall woman wearing fluorescent pink high-heels along with her business suit. We immediately created an atmosphere filled with humour. The people saw that I was prepared to laugh at myself. Within moments the people I needed to connect with realised that I did not fit the corporate stereotype most people have in the still male-dominated tech industry. The initial scepticism and passive aggression I faced originally now completely dissipated. Of course, I made sure that my credibility in terms of sales, the sales process, and the desired business outcomes we wanted from the changes were solid as a rock. But once our sales teams started to realise I knew what I was talking about *and* I was willing to listen to their views, my *pink shoes brand* took flight. I began to receive messages in anticipation of my visits, enquiring as to how they could help set the corporate changes to the sales processes in motion so that we could accelerate our anticipated success. I learned a valuable lesson in sales. This may have been focused on internal processes, but these teams still dealt with customers. And it matters not one jot where in the sales process you might be; the fact is that communication skills, coupled with a desire to succeed no matter how difficult the task may seem, are essential prerequisites for success."

Higher performers like Iris develop a growth mind-set that flavours their choices and actions during a sale. Salespeople with a growth mind-set see any challenge as an opportunity, and focus cheerfully on making the requisite effort with a *can-do* attitude. And while external factors not under their control can sometimes affect whether they ultimately win or fail, they spend less time ruminating over what's not in their power, and more time rolling up their sleeves where they *can* impact the outcome. By so doing, they create their own luck.

According to Jeff Raikes, CEO of the Bill & Melinda Gates Foundation, a growth mind-set is "key to closing the achievement gap." Growth-minded salespeople are enthusiastic to learn new things and go the extra mile to exceed their sales quotas. The salesperson with an attitude focused on growth takes care of their sales territory as if it was a mini-company and they were its CEO. They show total engagement and full accountability.

Colleen Schuller, Head of Global Selling Excellence at GlaxoSmithKline at the time of our research, told us: "When I started as a manager with GSK I was assigned to lead the worst sales territory in the region. It was at the very bottom. Yet, after 18 months it was one of the highest-selling areas. It took planning and hard work, but we completely turned that territory around. The only thing that really changed was my team's mind-set. They learned to believe we *could* win, and achieved better than anyone previously thought possible."

High-performing salespeople are constantly looking for new ways to add value to their clients, team and organization. They act as protagonists, focus on the real facts, ask hard questions, and get to the core of a performance issue. Thus, they learn from difficulties and outstretch their capabilities. In doing so, certain behaviours manifest themselves for people holding the Hero Journey Motivator for Control:

Most frequently observed behaviours
1. Convincing / Assuring
2. Persistent / Unrelenting
3. Self-reliant / Independent
4. Kind / Giving
5. Critical thinker

Top-performers categorically believe they are responsible for their own success. They thrive on challenge and see failure as a springboard. This growth mind-set holds that any person's current qualities can be improved. They subscribe to the notion that potential is limitless when you mix enough passion with training, toil, targets and time. Not only are growth-minded individuals not discouraged by failure, but they see themselves as having a learning experience in the process. "When I talk to my salespeople", says Justin Stone of J. P. Morgan, "I encourage them to forget that they are technically employed by a company. I ask them to imagine themselves as self-employed, running the whole show. If they were CEO of their own business and responsible for the client experience and all results, what might that do for their mind-set? I get a great reaction from people as it helps to shift mentality to one of total accountability. They see that this is their show, their destiny. It is at these times when people learn; and then they fly."

Top-performers believe they are equipped with a man-
date to create legacy. One high-performer who led a global
engagement project from 2000 to 2010 told us "during this
time, we became a regulated industry and a lot of challenges arose due to operating in this type of environment.
Making sure that things went well from a client perspective
and a regulator perspective was really hard," he told us.
Someone else might have given up, but he persevered: not
from a place of personal gratification but because he could
see the wider legacy that this project would create for his
firm. "I felt proudest on the day I handed things over to
my successor," he said with a smile, for this was his greatest
satisfaction. In 2014, Nike produced a motivational video
titled *Rise and Shine* through advertising agency lg2 Toronto.
Immediately going viral and now with millions of views, it
epitomizes the creed of salespeople with the Hero Journey
Motivator. It begins with that moment that many of us face
on those dark winter days when, "Your hand can't make
it to the alarm clock before the voices in your head start
telling you that it's too early, too dark, and too cold to get
out of bed." You know you want to push the button, to
steal just a few minutes more, but the hero within you wins
through and, wearily, you hit the streets, muscles aching and
protesting. You grind out the distance yard by yard. This is
the mark of the hero, the person in control; the person who
knows that they alone are responsible for their own destiny.

Heroes are not superhuman. As Nike said in their story,
while heroes are "not easily defeated, they are far from in-
vincible." There are those moments of self-doubt, of won-
dering if the prize is worth the fight, when the inner voices
seem to shout louder than the sound of the early morning
traffic. In these moments heroes are made. Heroes face up

to their own demons and refuse to accept that success is down to fate or chance. As Nike so elegantly put it, "Luck is the last dying wish of those who want to believe that winning can happen by accident. Sweat on the other hand is for those who know it's a choice."

In choosing to keep going on those days when the pressures of high-performing in an increasingly regulated world almost seemed insurmountable, he became a sales hero.

Harriet Taylor, working for Oracle at the time of our research, told us, "Every day I learn, or succeed, or a combination of both." Harriet is a sales hero.

Iconic salesperson Justin Stone of J. P. Morgan had this to say: "I read a lot of books and make my own notes. If I listen to an audiobook, I will listen to it once and then again to see how the ideas could work for me. It is a time investment. I think it is quite an important thing." Justin is a sales hero.

Phil Benton at Adidas suggests the following: "I value salespeople who show a degree of humility in comparing their actual achievements to their targets. Knowing where they are and what they need to change, they won't always succeed in the way you expect them to. They are the silent winners, and are highly respected." Phil's team members are sales heroes.

Microsoft's Dilip Mailvaganam adds that high-performers find themselves near the top of Maslow's hierarchy of needs[22] more often, achieve self-actualization, and so can look outward to meet the needs of others. Here's how he put it: "Whether it's helping the Guide Dogs for the Blind Association support people with sight loss, or using Kinect in the rehabilitation of children, or using the Cloud so Real Madrid can connect with 450 million fans, for me it's about using Microsoft technology to build a legacy that helps others. And the nice thing is that no one person can do it alone. It's not just me; it's not just my team; it's the collaboration of many teams which leads to success." Dilip, his team, and many others in Microsoft, are sales heroes.

The point of these practitioner vignettes is to illustrate how successful salespeople take control of their own affairs so their customers can gain better control over theirs. The more a salesperson means to their clients, the more their clients will mean to them. It's a virtuous circle.

———

On the next page is a worksheet for the Destination Belief of Control. Find a quiet place, contemplate the questions, and write down your responses. Doing so will move you along on the journey of applying the Salesperson's Secret Code. Following that, we provide additional insights about Control, which were shared by the iconic salespeople interviewed for our research.

MY CONTROL REVIEW

Q1. When something doesn't go as planned, who has final accountability?

Q2. Do you need others to give you praise? If so, why do you think that is?

Q3. Write down your talents. How long did you have to think about answering that question?

Q4. Who are your role models?

Q5. What was it like the last time you achieved something that put you outside your comfort zone? What new talents did you acquire? What did you learn about yourself?

ADDITIONAL CONTROL INSIGHTS FROM TOP-PERFORMING SALESPEOPLE

1. We know from the study that top-performers hold a belief that they intrinsically have all the resources they need within themselves and will make their own luck. Lower performers settle for a certain level of performance, but are less likely to "tempt the fates" by trying to step outside their designated lot in life. The former consistently accept full accountability for results; the latter accept only situational accountability, or none at all. If you believe you have everything you need to succeed, or have the shrewdness to find a way, you can achieve the seemingly impossible. A good start point is to change language patterns:

From:	To:
I have a bad sales patch to work. No one ever succeeds here.	*I have an opportunity to stand out like no one else has before. I will be the first to succeed here.*

2. Take ownership of mistakes regardless of your instinctive reaction. For example, imagine you are at a sales pitch and one of the pre-sales subject matter experts you bring in to demonstrate a product performs poorly in front of the customer. They aren't prepared and look disorganized. They don't speak in context to the customer's known business needs. They are so intent on narrating a canned presentation that they fail to hear when the customer tries to ask a question. As a result, you aren't invited through to the next round of the evaluation process, and don't win the sale. Is your colleague responsible or should you have taken ownership of briefing, training and rehearsing with them before the meeting began?

3. Top performers *always* seek feedback – the good, the bad and the ugly – so they can learn, develop, change and be more effective. They're not gluttons for criticism, but they can put it in the proper perspective when it comes their way. Low-performers abhor negative feedback, and have a ready response for why mitigating circumstances caused a less-than-ideal outcome. As they constantly point a finger outward at the world, they fail to see there are always three fingers pointing back in their own direction.

4. We found low-performers tend to use sales language that focuses on nuts-and-bolts tactical inputs like effort, activity, hours or cost. High-performers speak the language of strategic outputs, like revenue, margin, value, share of wallet and return on investment. High-performers also speak the language of empathy for their customers.

5. Those who accept accountability and focus on outputs are usually more frugal in their allocation of time. They tend to be surgical in the way they allocate tasks to the people most likely to achieve the desired result. They prefer not to leave things to chance. This doesn't mean they plan every iota of detail, but they do have a game plan, which they execute, gain feedback on and adapt as needed.

6. Remove ambiguity by agreeing on the scope of your accountability. You can't be accountable for things you have no control over. On the other hand, you must expose yourself to risk to stretch your capabilities, otherwise you won't push beyond the norm to deliver exceptional value. As American legal mind Oliver Wendell Holmes, Jr., wrote: "Man's mind, once stretched by a new idea, never regains its original dimensions." So, learn what you must do, decide to take control, be prepared to stretch, and go for it.

WHAT'S IN THE MIND?

The psychologist says...

Attribution theory is concerned with our interpretation of events. Internal attribution is where the cause of an individual's behaviour comes from within; it is rooted in personality, motives or beliefs. External attribution is where the cause of behaviour is assigned to an external environment outside one's control – for example, the economic environment. Our research suggests that if a salesperson uses internal attribution to reflect on success and failure, they can take ownership of the problem to resolve it or learn from it. Failure is therefore viewed as temporary and in a future situation they can manoeuvre successfully around it. This positive outlook can be adopted and coached by sales leaders to improve their salespersons' outlook in any situation.

The psychologist Julian B. Rotter developed the concept of *locus of control*. This can be a powerful tool for salespeople, sales leaders and organizations in considering where the power of control resides in any given situation. Think of this as a spectrum, with internal control at one end (an outcome of one's behaviour is dependent on one's own behaviour or personal characteristics) and external control (an outcome is a function of chance, luck or fate, is under the control of powerful others, or is simply unpredictable) at the other. Everyone will sit somewhere on that spectrum, perhaps varying with the situation in which the control is perceived. When talking about success and failure in a coaching situation (when sales targets have not been met or in a performance conversation, for example) explore this spectrum with the salesperson, recognizing what manoeuvre they can take in future to take control and lead themselves, and in turn the wider organization, to success.

THE LAST WORD
ON CONTROL

Banging the Drum of Destiny

Two young brothers, Bobby and David, wanted to be musicians. They pestered their parents almost daily about learning to play a variety of instruments. One day their father presented Bobby with a new guitar and announced that he would be having lessons. Bobby was thrilled.

It was David's birthday a couple of weeks later and he had asked for a drum kit. The special day arrived and, among the gifts, was a single, solitary drum: the sort you give to children to bang on, but most definitely not a drum kit. Bobby commiserated with David many times over the following days, as he practised on his shiny new guitar and began his lessons.

But David refused to be downhearted. He played that drum day in and day out. He played it along to music on the stereo system and he gave drum recitals to his parents and to Bobby. He began to invent new rhythms by drumming on the casing as well as on the drum skin.

Before long it was the holiday season and Christmas Day arrived. David came down to breakfast and the first gift he saw from his parents was a beautiful new drum kit, complete with bass, snare, cymbals and tom-toms. His mother smiled at him and said, "You have shown that you could make something of your desire to be a drummer. We were uncertain, but you showed such determination to teach yourself that we simply had to give you these drums for Christmas."

Over the years, Bobby played at playing his guitar. As for David, he went on to be taught by some of the greats and is a fabulous drummer to this day. Somehow, this is not in the least bit surprising.

Destination Belief
Someone or something must always be accountable for success (Control)

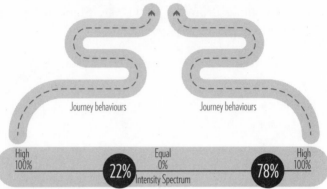

Journey behaviours   Journey behaviours

High 100%	Equal 0%		High 100%
	22% Intensity Spectrum	**78%**	

Journey Motivator 1
There is only so much
I can control (Victim)

Journey Motivator 2
I am ultimately responsible
for my own destiny (Hero)

50 percent of respondents believe they have a limited window of control over their sales, career, life or other people

100 percent of respondents who think there is only so much they can control also demonstrate intense fear of failure

Sales people are rewarded for winning. Whilst losing happens often, it's their wins that count above all else. This is called Casino Mentality. Some salespeople feel powerful—even lucky—in a familiar territory, yet powerless on new turf. Have you ever wondered why successful salespeople are the luckiest? The truth is they are not lucky; they have simply learned to attribute success and failure to themselves. Top performers control their destiny and see failure as a temporary detour not a destination—something to learn from and apply next time. In life, they succeed and learn (fail), but in order to continuously succeed they must continuously learn! Do you allow yourself the luxury to embrace failure in this way?

100 percent of respondents who think they are ultimately responsible for things that happen are high-performing

50 percent of respondents demonstrated strong internal locus of control

100 percent of respondents with strong internal locus of control were high-performing

CHAPTER
FOUR

RESILIENCE

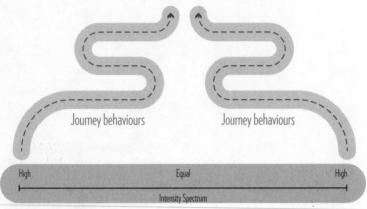

Destination Belief

Facing challenges and adversity are simply a fact of life (Resilience)

Journey behaviours | Journey behaviours

| High | Equal | High |

Intensity Spectrum

Journey Motivator 1
In the face of challenge
I work even harder and
win through (Work Hard)

Journey Motivator 2
I use moments of adversity
to find new and creative ways
to achieve goals (Work Smart)

Resilience is about how you withstand the impact of work and life events, including adversity, and your ability to get back on your feet again. Our wellbeing and resilience are built from a balance of expending energy during performance and taking time for renewal and recovery, thereby regaining energy. When stress arises, generally from demands or pressure for something that we care about, resilience helps us recover from the damage caused by it. Managing stress means acknowledging that it is happening and ushering in the restorative forces of healing and renewal, thereby rebuilding energy reserves.

Stress is one of the most demonized and misunderstood concepts in the world. People try to avoid it. However, stress is essential and vital to growth. And some stress, in the right situations, has a range of positive benefits. "Stress gives you the energy you need to rise to the challenge" (Kelly McGonigal, *The Upside of Stress*). Imagine that you are about to face a challenge. In that moment, your sympathetic nervous system swings into action. The body receives extra energy in the form of fat and sugar from the liver, and heart rate increases to ensure that all the nutrients, plus the additional oxygen being received from deeper breathing, arrive where they are needed. Adrenalin and cortisol are pumped into the bloodstream, together with endorphins and dopamine. As McGonigal, a psychologist and author, says, "Stress can create a state of concentrated attention … This side effect is one reason why some people enjoy stress – it provides a bit of a rush." Research also tells us that stress encourages us to become more socially minded because oxytocin – the hormone that helps us to connect with others, to show increased empathy, to listen more effectively – is released by the pituitary gland. This results in a *tend and befriend* response, quite different from the *flight or fight response* we have all heard about. This is all the more intriguing because oxytocin has been shown to dampen the fear response in the brain. It actually makes us feel braver.[23]

If stress can in fact be good for us, it seems that all too often the culprit of our ills is not excessive stress, but rather insufficient recovery. Stress is the stimulus for growth, and growth and resilience occur during episodes of recovery. When individuals do not properly honour the recovery process, the demands they face daily become insurmountable.

Inadequate emotional recovery causes negativity, mood swings and irritability. Inadequate mental recovery leads to poor concentration, sloppy thinking and mental mistakes. Spiritual fatigue not balanced by recovery can open the door to character lapses that conflict with your core values.

If you break an arm or a leg, there is a healing process that must occur to repair that injury so you can go forward with full functionality, and maybe even be stronger than you were before. That same process occurs emotionally, in our body, in our emotional mind, in our cognitive mind, and in our sense of purpose (the *what's it all about?* and *why am I here?* questions). Resilience speeds recovery. The stronger your resilience, the faster you can take a hit and move on. The key is to alternate times of stress with periods of recovery.

Resilience may be one of the most important cornerstones in our ability to navigate the new world we face, because we are constantly bombarded by things that knock us off our perch.

When 358 leaders in 190 companies were asked to identify their organizations' greatest performance obstacle, approximately 75% cited the ever-increasing demands of the workplace. Some 62% reported a rise in emotional or physical burnout over the previous 12 months, while 57% reported a significant drop in morale and 38% reported staff showing greater disengagement at work.[24]

When staff were asked about the impact of increased job demands, 63% reported being more irritated and stressed, and 56% were exercising less, which opens the door to increases in sedentary activity, obesity and related illnesses. Unsurprisingly, 69% reported a serious erosion of their ideal work/life balance. Most critically, 78% feared they personally lacked the capacity to deal with any additional challenge, setback or curve ball on top of what they were already handling.

Let's repeat that last statistic, because it's significant: nearly 80% of today's workers feel maxed out! This can lead to a rise in absenteeism (sick days, mental health days, etc.) as well as presenteeism (where people show up at work, and the lights are on, but *nobody's home*).

A recent Milken Institute study estimates that lost workdays and lower productivity costs businesses more than $1.3 trillion (USD) annually. Of this amount, lost productivity costs $1.1 billion (USD) per year, while another $2.7 billion (USD) is spent annually on treatment.[25]

With exercise declining and poor eating habits on the rise (think fast food, fad diets and energy drinks), we see chronic illnesses such as diabetes, cancer, obesity and cardiovascular disease add risk to businesses everywhere. Medical experts admit that 70% of all treatment costs is entirely preventable if people simply made small changes to their behaviour and beliefs, to achieve greater resilience.[26]

Emperor Napoleon Bonaparte of France was quoted as saying, "The first virtue in a soldier is endurance of fatigue; courage is only the second virtue."[27] He was talking about resilience. Physical fatigue in combat erodes cognitive, emotional and spiritual strength and is, therefore, the arch-enemy of high performance. Much of the training used by the military to improve resilience is relevant to the corporate world.

Swank and Marchand, doctors who studied the psychological impact of combat in World War II, found that after 60 consecutive days of fighting without respite, 98% of infantry soldiers are likely to become psychiatric casualties.[28] More recently, repeated military deployments to

Middle Eastern hotspots have underscored the importance of resilience as a protection against post traumatic stress disorder (PTSD). The military has learned the value, before redeploying soldiers, of a carefully administered dose of recovery between each stress cycle. The more traumatic the stress cycle, the more critical the periods of rest and recovery. The recovery phase is where emotional and physical stabilization occurs, and where resilience is created.

It's the same when you work out at the gym. Muscles don't grow while you're pumping iron. They grow when you're resting afterwards. What applies to the body applies equally to the mind. Here's how *Bodybuilder* magazine described it: "Not only does each muscle exercised need rest, i.e., *specific rest*, but so does the whole body, i.e., *general rest*. If rest for the whole body is not taken seriously too much stress can build up and lead the body into an over-trained state, due to the accumulation of stress. Not resting can slow down the body's recuperative ability and/or interrupt it; so, it is important that the whole body rests so it can be renewed with energy and vigor and allow the stress to dissipate. This is how the body [and mind] is kept strong and healthy and keeps growing."[29]

You might not serve in the military or hit the gym, but as a salesperson you're no stranger to basic training, going on campaigns 'in the field' and travelling across a territory. Whenever there is prolonged energy expenditure without breaks, the body allows it for a while, but ultimately responds with a backlash of forced recovery. Referred to as a parasympathetic backlash, this typically takes the form of overwhelming weariness, exhaustion, sleepiness and disengagement. If you spend your nights and mornings feeling exhausted from your sales job, you're not giving yourself enough recovery time and are likely to have low resilience. The good news is that you have the power to change this.

Military leaders know that one of the greatest dangers comes following a long and protracted campaign where there was no time for recovery during the battle. Immediately following the assault, soldiers typically become physiologically and psychologically compromised, making the entire unit vulnerable.

The continuous expenditure of energy eventually exhausts the body's capacity to produce energy, with the consequence being prolonged physical and emotional exhaustion. The body's energy-producing reserves simply burn out and take longer to recharge than if they'd been topped up along the way. The result: an involuntary shutdown.

This is survival-based and is a form of forced recovery to preserve life. One way this manifests itself is through people falling into an involuntary deep sleep despite needing to stay alert. Have you ever jerked awake while you were working on your laptop late at night? Or in the middle of the afternoon? The reason for this debilitating fatigue is an absence of even short cycles of energy recovery and restoration.

The key to building resilience is to incorporate strategic recovery in your life. In businesses that haven't been educated on the power of resilience, the notion of taking breaks for renewal and regeneration can be a hard pill to swallow. Taking breaks may be perceived as a sign of weakness. "Breaks are for wimps" can be a prevailing attitude among hard-charging tactical sales managers. However, without question, cycles of stress must be balanced with cycles of recovery if resilience is to be built and sustained.

Enlightened companies are starting to understand. For example, North Carolina-based SAS is the world's largest privately owned software company, employing more than 14,000 people worldwide. CEO Jim Goodnight is a contrarian leader who believes in giving staff a challenge, but also encourages downtime for recovery. SAS offers flexible hours to take care of family, healthy eating options to keep concentration levels high, full fitness facilities and manicured grounds for games and sport.[30]

SAS's generous provision of healthcare, childcare, education and other mechanisms to maintain its human capital is something most CFOs would baulk at, but the results speak for themselves. Now in its fourth decade of double-digit sales growth, boasting better than 90% customer retention and among the lowest staff churn in its industry, SAS consistently ranks among the world's top ten best places to work.[31]

Results like these demonstrate how the body's need for resilience is business-relevant. Most organizations hire people for the "software" in their minds; all their intelligence, wisdom and genius. However, that software lies dormant if the machine isn't plugged in and its battery restored on a regular basis.

Phil Benton of Adidas doesn't think it is possible to succeed without it. He told us, "I've gone through many bumps in the road and learned from all of them. You build resilience. I am a better sales manager because of it."

Every salesperson we spoke to in our study believed facing challenges and adversity is a normal fact of life. Supporting this Destination Belief are two Journey Motivators, as detailed in the previous two chapters.

The first Journey Motivator, "In the face of challenge

I work even harder and win through," is summed up by *Work Hard*.

The second Journey Motivator, "I use moments of adversity to find new and creative ways to achieve goals," recognizes that adversity encourages problem solving, and is summed up by *Work Smart*.

We found every high-performing salesperson held the Work Smart sub-belief more intensely than Work Hard.

Destination belief: Facing challenges and adversity is simply a fact of life (Resilience)

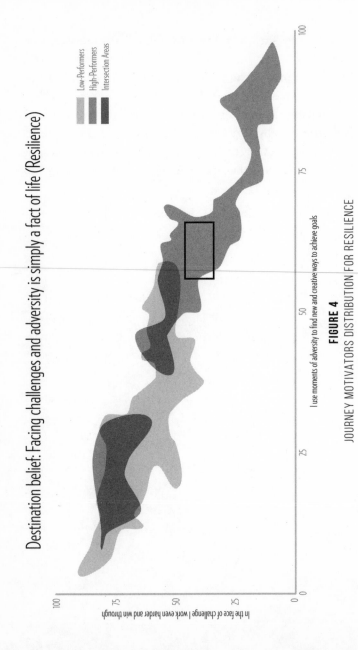

Low-Performers
High-Performers
Intersection Areas

In the face of challenge I work even harder and win through

I use moments of adversity to find new and creative ways to achieve goals

FIGURE 4

JOURNEY MOTIVATORS DISTRIBUTION FOR RESILIENCE

Our research found the optimal position for Resilience is 59% *Work Smart* and 41% *Work Hard*. When analysing the very best of the best (the top 5% of high-performing salespeople interviewed), we noticed a cluster, identified by the rectangle in *Figure 4*. It confirms top salespeople do hold both Journey Motivators, but they subscribe to *Work Smart* more than twice as often as other salespeople. Let's explore both Journey Motivators in more detail.

JOURNEY MOTIVATOR 1:
'IN THE FACE OF CHALLENGE I WORK EVEN HARDER AND WIN THROUGH.'
(WORK HARD)

Pioneering automaker Henry Ford once said, "When everything seems to be going against you, never forget that the airplane takes off against the wind, not with it."[32] The sales game can be like that. Success comes after powering through adversity and rejection. Mild bouts of negativity may be difficult to deal with at times, but top salespeople do more than cope with it, they thrive on it. Yet that doesn't mean they work harder.

In our research, 91% of low-performing salespeople said they believed they *had to* work harder to win their deals. They hold on to the idea that if they just put in the hours, a solution will develop even when one isn't immediately evident. They keep on going, doing the same thing, with a hope that circumstances will change, Providence will shine, and an answer will appear. Let's not follow this perceived wisdom.

One said: "When I face a challenge I go into sixth gear, dig deep and use my inner conviction to power through.' Another put it this way: "Rewards go to the hard-working". Other pieces of wisdom included: "You need to be the first one in the office and the last one still plugging away after midnight, when your competition is asleep." We might well hear an echo of Gordon Gekko, from the movie *Wall Street*, chiding: "You win some, you lose some, but you keep on fighting ... and if you need a friend, get a dog."

By contrast, only 14% of high-performing salespeople were found to have similar beliefs.

We recognize that industrious mantras don't sound like low performance. They make people sound like they're pumped up and destined to do well. But here is the surprising contradiction: devotees of Work Hard do so because they aren't actually in control. It's the equivalent of throwing darts at a target and hoping something sticks.

"Powering through" into the wee hours really means you haven't managed your work day wisely, and are prepared to rob your personal or family time as a penalty, which may skew other parts of your life out of balance. The behaviour gets dressed up as a testosterone-soaked, caffeine-fuelled vigil, a tribute of loyalty to the firm. But it's just bad self-management.

Remember, doing more of the same thing is rarely the solution. If this were true, Henry Ford would have created faster horses and not cars. It should therefore not surprise you that working harder in the face of challenge rarely brings success.

You may have heard of Arthur Miller's 1949 play, *Death of a Salesman*, which won numerous Tony Awards and a Pulitzer Prize. It is widely considered to be one of the greatest plays of the 20th century.[33] The script portrays a well-meaning salesperson, Willy Loman, exhausted after a cancelled business trip, remembering career and life decisions that led him to financial and moral bankruptcy. It's a classic tale of someone who worked hard, not smart, then burned out with nothing to show for it.

If your response to adversity is to work harder and longer, not smarter, certain behaviours will manifest themselves. The more intensely the Work Hard Journey Motivator is held, the more exaggerated these behaviours become. Let's review the frequently occurring behavioural traits of people holding the Work Hard Journey Motivator for Resilience:

Most frequently observed behaviours
1. Persistent / Unrelenting
2. Outspoken / Free-speaking
3. Strong-willed / Forceful
4. Brave / Fearless
5. Stubborn / Immoveable

Remember, these behaviours – on their own – can lead to lower sales performance when compared with the top-performers in our study. The alternative is to Work Smart as well.

The most successful people do work hard, but also in an exceptionally smart way. They maintain the same level of persistence and drive while considering ways to do things differently. Working harder without taking the time to work smarter is an easy habit to slip into.

The late Stephen Covey, author of the bestselling *Seven Habits of Highly Effective People* (Free Press, 2004), told a story about a woodcutter whose saw grows blunt as time passes. He has much work to do, and doesn't want to step away to sharpen his tool. But if he were to stop, sharpen his saw, and go back to cutting with a sharp blade, he would save time and effort. Covey wrote: "Sharpen the Saw means preserving and enhancing the greatest asset you have – you. It means having a balanced programme for self-renewal in the four areas of your life: physical, social/emotional, mental and spiritual."

JOURNEY MOTIVATOR 2: 'I USE MOMENTS OF ADVERSITY TO FIND NEW AND CREATIVE WAYS TO ACHIEVE GOALS.' *(WORK SMART)*

Why do some salespeople bloom in adversity, yet others wither? A significant differentiator of high-performing salespeople is that they use moments of adversity to find new, creative ways to achieve their goals.

We found that 86% of high-performing salespeople fall into this group.

Dr Jim Loehr is a world-renowned tennis pro turned sports performance psychologist, and cofounder of the Florida-based Human Performance Institute. In the 1980s he studied the world's elite tennis players, looking for what separated the great competitors from the runners-up. What sets his work apart is that he focused on an aspect of the game that had been traditionally ignored: the nearly 70% of the time during a match when the players aren't even on court.

He became convinced that the way players use their non-playing time is what separates champions from losers. He drew this conclusion by watching hundreds of hours of videotapes of top players, where he saw almost no difference between competitors at play. Between points, however, the top players followed rituals the others didn't, and they did so on a highly consistent basis.

Ritual One is that after the point ends, the player who lost the point will immediately swing the racquet again and replay the shot as it should have been. They put their body and mind through the paces of what success looks like, and carry that thought with them as they move to the next position. This way their most recent self-image isn't of a failure, but of a success.

Ritual Two is when the player walks to the backcourt with their head held high, back straight, exuding energy and confidence (whether they feel it or not). They know every negative reaction will deplete more energy than will a positive one. Winners don't waste their energy.

Ritual Three is recovery, when the player continues walking to the baseline or umbrella-chair. Here they go into a mini-meditation of deep breathing, contracting and relaxing muscles to stay loose, and keeping their eyes focused on the strings of their racquet to minimize visual distraction. Their goal here is to relax and allow time for physical and mental recovery.

Ritual Four is the only time between points where conscious thought plays a role. They step back to the baseline, strike a confident pose, and give themselves a pep talk.

Finally, Ritual Five is when players visualize hitting the ball to a specific target, or breaking their opponent's service in a specific way. Here they follow an unvarying set of acts (such as repeated ball bouncing or twirling the racquet) to put their brain back in the groove.[34]

Eight-time Grand Slam champion Andre Agassi "was the best at managing the between-point time of any athlete

I'd seen," Loehr said. "If you go back and look, no matter whether he hit a winner or missed three balls in a row… you honestly couldn't tell if he had lost the point or won it. He would follow his routine 100%: the walk, the movement of the eyes, it was absolutely the best."[35]

The next time you watch Wimbledon, thank Loehr for the increasing trend of nigh-orgasmic grunting when players serve the ball. He noticed the best players exhale deeply and rhythmically as they hit the ball. They employ an aspect of recovery that allows the player to let go, release tension and loosen their muscles to improve resilience. Lesser players tend to hold their breath and store their stress, which eventually fatigues the body.

The insight at the heart of Loehr's work is that what you think determines how you feel, and those emotions have physical consequences. Psychology affects physiology. The cycle is self-reinforcing: anxiety compromises the body, leading to poor play, and poor play in turn prompts more anxiety. It is simply not possible to play your best if you're thinking negatively. However, people with greater resilience model positive emotions, bounce back faster, and go on to win more often.

Which behaviour traits were consistent across each interview transcript and the corresponding behavioural model for people holding to the Work Smart Journey Motivator for Resilience?

Most frequently observed behaviours
1. Expressive
2. Decisive / Firm
3. Even-tempered / Calm
4. Restless / Moving
5. Strong-willed / Forceful

Salespeople who use moments of adversity to find new and creative ways to achieve goals are more successful, more of the time. They begin with an attitude that every problem is an opportunity to shine.

This view is consistent with most high-performing salespeople, including Phil Benton of Adidas, who suggests that there's a solution to every problem if you get creative enough. Phil faced a huge challenge in 2012 when he was tasked with delivering his company's role in the London Olympics, at the same time as managing his sales team. With limited resources, and a long list of tasks to complete, several logistical challenges presented themselves.

'We had almost no time and few resources,' he recalls. "It was far from ideal. So, I encouraged staff to think of three options for each challenge, and debate which one was *the least worst option*. After taking each action, we ran after-action reviews on what went wrong, but focused more on what went well – so we could repeat successful methods in upcoming tasks."

In a time-poor setting, accepting the least worst option meant people weren't hung up on seeking perfection. By subtly replacing the term "success review" with after-action review, the language focused people on *doing*. As General George S. Patton Jr. said while commanding the US Seventh Army in Europe during World War II, "A good plan violently executed now is better than a perfect plan executed next week."[36]

One piece of advice from Louis Jordan, formerly Vice-Chairman at Deloitte, is to look for opportunities when others are looking at threats. He told us, "Significant change is now occurring regularly across once traditional industries. As disruptive and divisive as these changes may be and are, they do represent opportunity to provide advice because there is a lot of uncertainty. When there is uncertainty, there are a lot of questions asked. As worrisome as it may be to some, individually and some at a corporate level, I think of it as a good opportunity to get closer to clients and help them through uncertain times. If you are able to answer their questions you are in a very favourable position. So, when there is a change in your market or industry, remember this is a very a good opportunity for you to provide advice and guidance. Granted, you may face rejection but you build your reputation as a source of future counsel."

Our research indicates that telesales people face rejection more than any other sales role. On average, they dial 100 contacts per shift, which amounts to 2,000 dial-outs per month. They have "meaningful conversations" with 14%, which includes talking to the target contact, or others who give advice on who the right person is. Of these 280 conversations held each month, around 3.5% (ten per month) get reported as qualified sales opportunities in the pipeline. Once here, the typical win rate is 30% (3 wins per month). End-to-end, telesales people face a 99.9985% failure rate.[37] And that requires a high level of resilience.

Psychologists from Johnson & Johnson's Health and Wellness Solutions division suggest four tips for boosting personal resilience:

1. **Use Stress to Your Advantage**

   "There are several types of stress, not all of which are bad," explains Raphaela F. O'Day, Ph.D., senior manager, Strategic Health Content, Behavioural Science, Johnson & Johnson Health and Wellness Solutions. "We believe that there is a great opportunity to help people identify the different kinds in their lives and reframe how they think about – and act upon – them."

   So how, exactly, do you do that? By tweaking your thinking to view stress not as an obstacle, but as a tool for growth. As Louis Jordan says, "Working in a variety of tough sales environments provides you with a resilience that you need. You gain the ability to treat success and failure as the same – to use any failure as an enquiry of learning. You might not win today, but by not winning you do not automatically lose. There is no set piece to winning, you might have to rebuild and go again, but that's the fun of it. One of the best pieces of advice I ever had was from a former boss. We were in one of those situations where you pick the wrong option and things did not go well. He said, that sometimes you zig when you should have zagged; just learn and move on."

   Consider work situations that send your tension levels skyrocketing. Do you hate saying "no" to your superiors, or giving negative feedback to colleagues? Instead of avoiding or delegating such tasks to other people, actively challenge yourself to do them when the need arises.

It may feel uncomfortable at first, but with practice you can develop your capacity to better handle those moments – and acquire skills in the process that can serve you well in any workplace.

2. **Make Recovery Time a Priority**

Let's say you've been working 80-hour weeks for the past three months. Not surprisingly, that kind of intense schedule can cause excessive stress and fatigue. And yet most hard-charging personalities don't give themselves the time – or, perhaps, the permission – to truly take a rest occasionally. "Recovery is regarded as a weakness," says Jennifer Lea, a Johnson & Johnson performance coach. "Everybody is stressed out; everyone has to drive hard."

What's more, when most people hear the word "recovery" they tend to think of passive pursuits, like long walks on the beach or a guilt-ridden afternoon bingeing on recorded TV shows – activities that may not appeal to those who prefer to go, go, go 24/7.

But low-key activities aren't the only way to reinvigorate and re-energize. Vigorous exercise – be it a brisk jog or a spin class – can also be great for helping to reboot and redirect your tired brain. Bottom line: Lea says that whatever works best for you, "those are the things you should seek to do regularly to help with these periods of stress we all face."

3. **Differentiate Ongoing Stress from Occasional Stress**

Stressors come in many insidious shapes and forms. Think about the biggest sources in your life. Are they chronic, everyday annoyances, like a finicky child who refuses to eat every night, or a coworker who habitually drops the ball? Or is it something with an end date, such as planning a wedding or an important work presentation?

Once you determine the type of stress you're facing, you can then figure out how to best manage, minimize or get through it. "Stress with strategic recovery allows us to grow incrementally and therefore become more resilient to the challenges we face," explains Lea.

Translation: tailor your recovery time to the type of burdens you're currently encountering. If they're the ongoing kind, make a point of scheduling regular and recurring chunks of downtime on your calendar. But if you know they'll be over by a certain point, keep your eyes on the prize and plan serious recovery time as a reward at the end. Hello, vacation!

4. **Reframe How You Think About Failure**

Much like stress, failure at some point in life is not just normal, but inevitable. So, the next time you get something wrong at work, don't view it as a character flaw or a sign that you're incapable and underqualified. See it as an opportunity to learn from your mistakes.

If you've missed an important deadline, for instance, think about how you can better manage your time to make the next one promptly. Or if you blanked out on showing up for a meeting, figure out what calendar alerts or reminders you can put in place so it doesn't happen again.

In other words, instead of berating yourself, focus on recovering quickly from failure and how to make better decisions in the future to help you avoid it. "That," says Lea, "is the [true] measure of resilience."[38]

The fact is that no one is perfect and we are often our own worst critics. It may come hard to some people, but having the courage to reach out to other people and say that you need help can work wonders. "A problem shared is a problem halved," says the old proverb. How many of us can look in the mirror and truthfully say that the person looking back at us has the strength of character to do that as often as we could?

———

On the next page is a worksheet for the Destination Belief of Resilience. Find a quiet place, contemplate the questions, and write down your responses. Doing so will help you along the journey of applying the Salesperson's Secret Code. Following that, we provide additional insights about Resilience, which were shared by the iconic salespeople interviewed for the research.

MY RESILIENCE REVIEW

Q1. Are you a "grit your teeth" person or do you optimistically rise to the challenges of life? What balance of both do you observe in yourself? What examples can you draw upon?

Q2. How do you continuously develop your personal network in the good times so that when things go wrong you have a ready-made support group?

Q3. Do you regard times of adversity as moments to "buck the trend" or "keep your head down?"

Q4. How do you react emotionally to periods of challenge and adversity? What might this tell you?

ADDITIONAL RESILIENCE INSIGHTS FROM TOP-PERFORMING SALESPEOPLE

1. Most of us are familiar with the experience of silently talking to ourselves in our head. This is a phenomenon psychologists call 'inner speech'. People hear words (usually in their own accent), or see ideas come as images, feelings or downloads of fully-formed thoughts. It varies. Our inner speech can lift us or berate us. Top performers keep this voice upbeat. If it voices criticism, they decide whether it's constructive and warranted. If so, they listen and learn. If it sounds more like fear and limiting beliefs, they reframe the dialogue as follows:

Limiting belief	Behaviour it drives	Reframed belief	Behaviour it drives
This sales call is going to be difficult.	• Cautious • Defensive • Pessimistic	*This sales call is my chance to outshine the others.*	• Creative • Optimistic • Brave
Today's meeting will be boring.	• Weary • Downbeat • Dreamy	*Today's meeting is key to propel me forwards.*	• Energetic • Enthusiastic • Visionary
I'm not going to win this deal.	• Depressed • Fearful • Resigned	*I know how to navigate to the finish line.*	• Excited • Eager • Challenged

FIGURE 5
REFRAMING THE INNER DIALOGUE

2. Draw strength from the times when you're at your best. Remember a sales scenario that went incredibly well. Visualize how you acted, what you said and how it felt. Recall how you prepared logically and emotionally. Respect your ability to hit the high notes. If you did it once before, you can do it again. Every time. Today. If you're new to sales, remember yourself in a different setting doing extraordinary work. Treasure this as a candle to shine when you feel lost in the dark.

3. Build greater resilience by balancing your physical and emotional wellbeing:
   a. **Your Body:** What you eat, how you sleep, your exercise programme, work/life balance, rest and recuperation.
   b. **Your Cognitive Mind:** How you keep learning and process your experiences. How you relate to the world around you.
   c. **Your Emotional Mind:** Understand what triggers your negative emotions – break the pattern; rewrite the script. How you recognize your unique talents and channel these into a positive state of wellbeing.
   d. **Your Purposeful Mind:** Knowing your values, moral code and life purpose; establishing rituals to achieve balance.

4. In times of change and challenge, consider the axiom, "A problem shared is a problem halved." Crowdsource your challenges. By working collaboratively with others, you can share talents, perspectives and experiences. Let their input energize you. Some salespeople corral colleagues into a room. Others make calls or send emails to their mentors. It's an increasingly popular practice to post business challenges on LinkedIn or Quora (just make sure you don't mention clients, bosses or adversaries by name).

5. Resilience and vitality can be damaged when you have nothing to do. Boredom is an environment that allows the harbingers of doom to have a field day. Fill your day proactively with plans, actions, bite-size goals and plenty of small wins. Live your life with purpose and gain a greater sense of fulfilment so that when those hard moments arrive (as they surely will) you are ready to bounce back quickly.

WHAT'S IN THE MIND?

The psychologist says...

The brain is a fascinating and still relatively unknown organ. And yet, the more we learn about how it works – the cause and effect of impulses generated within it upon our mental and physical wellbeing – the more we are learning that the mind and body are indeed part of the same integrated, interdependent system. Of course, there are plenty of religious scholars around who will tell you that their values and beliefs embodied this literally thousands of years ago. They are probably quite right!

In his seminal work *Why Zebras Don't get Ulcers*, Dr Robert Sapolsky illustrates how constantly raised levels of anxiety, of adrenalin and cortisol in the bloodstream, and increased heart rate, all cause stress. This is either going to save you from the lions or won't do long-term harm because you will be lunch. We carry those basic fight-or-flight patterns into our modern business world and, unlike the zebras, we forget to switch them off. The result is a downward spiral of performance.[39]

The American Psychological Society describes resilience as "the process of adapting well in the face of adversity, trauma, tragedy, threats or significant sources of stress, such as family and relationship problems, serious health problems or workplace and financial stressors. It means bouncing back from difficult experiences." A natural reaction of many people in stressful environments, such as sales, is to work through the challenge or difficulty – run faster, make more calls, pitch harder, etc. This may well have a positive effect if the individual has the capacity.

Working harder is certainly a part of the answer. Sales-people and sales leaders will benefit from open and honest conversations when extra effort is a potential solution in tough times.

The top-performing salespeople also work smarter. Part of that "smartness" comes from the way they process what is happening to them and around them, which gives them more choices than simply running harder to stand still. Here are five ways salespeople and leaders can create an environment where *smart* has a better chance of winning the day:

1. **Be realistic – recognize a "threat" early.** Don't enter a stage of denial. Be honest with yourself about what is happening. This is smart behaviour.

2. **Manage your emotional state.** Panicked and rash reactions do not help, but a period of pausing, reflecting, being open and then accepting can enable calm and rational evaluation. New ideas and new plans will emerge and a state of "renewal" is created. That's smart.

3. **Identify the "good intent" in your current difficulties.** Resilient people will look for the possible good in their situation. For example, business is bad and customers are few. The "good intent" might be that you will be encouraged to seek new markets, change the product, alter pricing, etc. In short, from adversity comes innovation… and that's clever.

4. **Share your pain.** The fact is that people who have a wide, trusted network are more likely to come through

a difficult period than those who have no one to fall back on. This means that we should be ready and able to show empathy for others when they hit tough times. When it's our turn you might be surprised how many want to offer help and support. Sharing is a smart move.

5. **Look after yourself more than ever.** Champion athletes need rest and proper diet to complement their exercise regime. Salespeople are no different. We don't expect Usain Bolt to win the 100 metres running on empty. Success begins with self-respect, and part of that is about looking after you. What's not smart about that?

THE LAST WORD ON RESILIENCE

This is a popular and often-told story. We don't know where it comes from, but we love it and want to share its message with you.

Potatoes, Eggs or Coffee?

Once upon a time a daughter complained to her father that her life was hard and she didn't know how she was going to overcome the challenges she was facing. The daughter was tired of fighting day in and day out. It seemed that just as one problem was solved, another one soon followed. Her inner dialogue was very limiting.

Her father, a chef, took her to the kitchen. He filled three pans with water and placed each one on the stove. Once the pans began to boil, he placed potatoes in the first, eggs in the second and ground coffee beans in the third.

He let them sit and boil, without saying a word to his daughter. The daughter moaned and groaned, becoming impatient with this crazy exercise.

After 20 minutes, the father turned off the burners. He took the potatoes out of the pan and placed them in a bowl. He pulled the eggs out and placed them in a bowl. He then ladled the coffee into a cup. Turning to his daughter, he asked, "What do you see?"

"Potatoes, eggs and coffee," she hastily replied.

"Look closer," he said, "and touch the potatoes." The girl did so and noticed that they were soft. He then asked her to take an egg and break it. After pulling off the shell, she revealed the hard-boiled egg underneath. Finally, he invited his daughter to taste the coffee. As she did the full flavours and the aroma made her feel so good.

"Father, what does this mean?" she asked. He then explained that the potatoes, the eggs and the coffee beans had all faced the same challenge – the boiling water. However, each one reacted differently.

The potato went in strong, hard and unrelenting, but in boiling water it became soft and weak.

The egg was fragile, with the shell protecting its soft inside until it was put in the boiling water. Then the inside became hardened.

However, the ground coffee beans were different. After they were exposed to the boiling water, they changed the water. They created something new and entirely different.

"Which are you," the man asked his daughter. "When the going gets tough for you, how do you respond? Are you a potato, an egg or a coffee bean?"

Destination Belief
Facing challenges and adversity are simply a fact of life (Resilience)

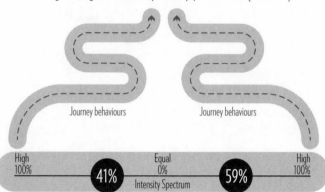

Journey behaviours | Journey behaviours

High 100% | 41% | Equal 0% | 59% | High 100%

Intensity Spectrum

Journey Motivator 1
In the face of challenge
I work even harder and
win through (Work Hard)

Journey Motivator 2
I use moments of adversity
to find new and creative ways
to achieve goals (Work Smart)

91 percent of all
salespeople said they
believed they had to work
harder to win their deals

Telemarketers face a
99.9985 percent failure
rate, higher than any
other type of selling

Working harder can be an easy habit to slip into, though. Stephen Covey tells a story about a woodcutter whose saw gets blunter as time passes and he continues cutting down trees. If the woodcutter were to stop sawing, sharpen his saw and go back to cutting the tree with a sharp blade, he would actually save time and effort in the long run. The analogy is an easy one to remember but harder to put into practice. Here's what Covey says about sharpening the saw in your life. "Sharpen the Saw means preserving and enhancing the greatest asset you have--you. It means having a balanced program for self-renewal in the four areas of your life: physical, social/emotional, mental and spiritual." Sharpening your saw is a great habit to get into in all areas of your life, but we think it can be especially beneficial when it relates to resilience.

95 percent of low performers believe that 'circumstances sometimes conspire against them'

83 percent of high performers continuously develop their personal network in the good times so that when things go wrong they have a ready-made support group

93 percent of high performers can articulate why they do what they do

CHAPTER
FIVE

INFLUENCE

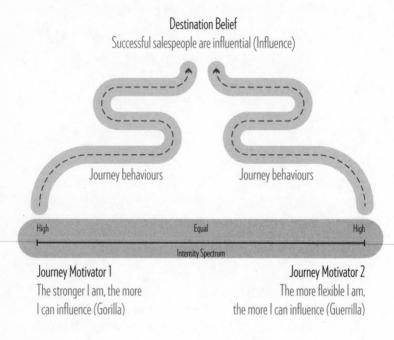

Destination Belief
Successful salespeople are influential (Influence)

Journey behaviours   Journey behaviours

High   Equal   High
Intensity Spectrum

Journey Motivator 1
The stronger I am, the more
I can influence (Gorilla)

Journey Motivator 2
The more flexible I am,
the more I can influence (Guerrilla)

Every salesperson we spoke to in our research believes successful salespeople use influence and persuasion to open doors, collect information and gain commitment. They persuade prospects to see a need they didn't recognize before, to feel an urge to act quickly, and to have a preference of supplier.

At the same time as they're working to influence customers, top sellers also work internally to influence bosses and colleagues. Ask across departments to learn what people think of an influential salesperson, and you'll hear they relate to them culturally, like them socially, value them commercially. They're willing to help that salesperson achieve their goals by offering special resources, pricing or time extensions not generally given to others. This bestowal of goodwill has nothing to do with favouritism, tenure or formal rank. It's all achieved through influence. Again and again, our interview transcripts cited examples of top-performers being aware that they have this impact and are not afraid to make the most of it.

Such persuaders are opinionated enough to see the world as they want it to be. They have a knack for getting close to others who can help put the pieces together, then influencing those people to make it happen.

At first glance, Influence can look a lot like its darker cousin, *manipulation*, so we need to understand the Journey Motivators that support and differentiate it as an ethical element for professional selling.

We can look at the following two Journey Motivators in terms of a *Gorilla* mind-set (the muscle-bound primate getting what he wants through brute force) vs. a *Guerrilla* perspective (irregular fighters who engage in battle using clever, unconventional means).

The first Journey Motivator supporting this part of the code is that influence is achieved through *Formal* means. This is when the salesperson asserts their authority or title, their reputation, their corporate brand power or testimonials to make new prospects feel they're in safe hands, and think twice about buying from anyone else. They tend to target conversations with the highest formal officer they can reach in the customer's business. They believe that influence starts at the head and flows downwards from a position of strength. It's about being the most dominant *Gorilla*, where "the stronger I am, the more I can influence."

The second Journey Motivator is that influence is achieved through *Informal* means. This is where the seller doesn't depend on (or may not have) a dominant brand or reputation, and doesn't focus solely on high-level customer contacts. Instead, these salespeople work as prolific networkers, are attentive to many people's needs, and seek to make a fresh contribution instead of defining themselves by past achievements.

They network low as well as high, to make sure they're talked about positively by as many people as possible. This is because, from the outside of a customer's business, they have no way of knowing at first who the opinion leaders are. So, they marshal partisans and allies in many departments, at all levels.

This works because somewhere inside that company are people with influence over diaries and decisions. They're part of the club – that cadre of people who decide what value looks like, what culture will pervade the business, what behaviour is acceptable, and where the company or department should go next. They pull the strings, and are at the centre of the informal network.

You're sure to have seen these people before. They're the ones who join a meeting late without criticism, while others are reprimanded for being tardy. They're the person others defer to in a meeting and ask, "What do you think?" before a decision is made – yet they seem to hold no apparent authority. They're the folks who somehow manage to hire new staff during a hiring freeze. They get resources when others get none. They may or may not be the longest-serving employee. Their business card may or may not have a senior title. Yet whatever station they hold, people treat them differently. They're connected, powerful.

At first glance, you can't possibly know who they are, and it's unlikely your first entrée to a company will be through the most influential person. So, it's wise to land and expand: once you're through the gate, connect to multiple people and plant your flag. Keep prospecting. Make connections. Lower-performers did not speak with the same intensity as the high-performers about the need to expand their network, their influence. The higher-performers seemed to enjoy the challenge of ascending the "mountain of influence." As they climb this mountain, they make sure they have plenty of anchor points; if one mooring comes loose, the others will catch them.

Are there any tests you can run to know which contacts have influence? Of course there are! Test if people's actions go beyond their words, or if they promise much but deliver little. You might ask for an email address, an introduction, next year's strategic plan, or a company organization chart. Just make sure you ask for *something* and see if they tell you it's impossible, or if they shrug and get it done. Low-performers worry that asking such things will "push their luck," so they tend to ask less. Top sellers make their own luck: many in the top-performing group said that they test the pull of others by asking for things only a person of influence can deliver. Then they know.

When you reach people who provide evidence that they are in the company's inner circle, show whose side you're on – *theirs*. Your intent is to contribute to their business or to their personal ambition. Show you can take them from where they are today to where they've decided to go in the future. Be their bridge. When you position yourself thus, they'll do most of your selling for you because it's in their interests to help you.

This is a little bit of politics and a little bit of influence. It's certainly not the rigid, top-down hierarchical approach people follow when their belief system fixates on the flow of formal strength (Journey Motivator 1). No, this is the battle plan used by the *Guerrilla* who embraces Journey Motivator 2, where "the more flexible I am, the more I can influence." They know that, in order to connect with people of influence in the customer organization, they need to be seen as a person of influence in their own organization and beyond.

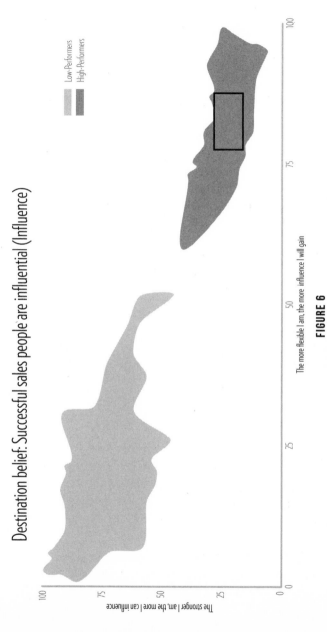

Destination belief: Successful sales people are influential (Influence)

Low-Performers
High-Performers

The more flexible I am, the more influence I will gain

The stronger I am, the more I can influence

FIGURE 6

JOURNEY MOTIVATORS DISTRIBUTION FOR INFLUENCE

Our research found that top salespeople are driven by both of these Journey Motivators, but *Guerrilla* influence is applied three times more frequently than *Gorilla* power when the top-performers are out selling. The optimal position for Influence therefore is 74% *Guerrilla* and 26% *Gorilla*. Let's explore the Journey Motivators in more detail.

JOURNEY MOTIVATOR 1:
'THE STRONGER I AM, THE MORE I CAN INFLUENCE.' *(GORILLA)*

According to the salespeople who hold this Journey Motivator, there's value in getting up early, staying late at the office, holding all-nighters to prep pitches for the next day, being assertive, and pressing on after hearing "No" multiple times. They aim to get their brief from the highest-ranking customer contact, and then work down from the top. They tend to provoke the customer to confront their issues or see their inadequacies. They then use challenging questions and present compelling alternatives to the status quo, which establishes the seller as a force to be reckoned with, a thought leader, a force to be taken seriously.

Salespeople who live by this Journey Motivator know their subject matter backwards. They are product experts and business issue gurus who pride themselves on being skilled at leading the customer through several tollgates of inquiry, having the "right" answers for them, and being fluid at narrating the slideware issued by their Marketing department.

These salespeople tell themselves that using challenging questions proves they possess the expertise to be trusted, as well as showing a genuine desire to truly understand the customer's situation. Multiple salespeople in this group told us, "Asking challenging questions shows my customer that I know what I am talking about, makes them really stop and think, and so helps me establish credibility for the solution I'm presenting."

This Journey Motivator is rooted in an appreciation of the power of persuasion, and manifests itself as passion for the product or service being sold.

However, 56% of salespeople who embrace this Journey Motivator with a high intensity are low-performers!

This finding is a bombshell because it seems to contradict several decades of modern sales training that has sought to teach business-to-business (B2B) salespeople to ask better questions, to help the customer connect the dots. It's not a matter of this direction being flawed, but rather it reveals a problem in its execution.

Too many salespeople still come across as dogmatic and manipulative. They display the artifice of listening to the customer, but are only waiting for their turn to talk again. Their passion to convince, persuade or even coerce becomes the end that justifies the means. The conversation becomes less about mutual discovery, and more about imposing their beliefs (or their products) on the customer.

Buyers say they come away from these encounters impressed by the seller's commitment to what they're selling, and often better educated with interesting titbits and statistics from the seller. Still, they confess to feeling harassed and even insulted by what can come across as a superior attitude or talk-fest on the part of the salesperson. Some felt it bordered on negligence, with the salesperson failing to grasp the customer's needs because the questions were hollow and the listening almost non-existent.

But at first glance, these sellers don't look like low-performers. See below the behaviour traits that are consistent across each interview transcript and the corresponding behavioural model we collected from people with a high-intensity Gorilla Journey Motivator for Influence:

Most frequently observed behaviours
1. Aggressive / Challenger
2. Persistent / Tenacious
3. Daring / Risk-taker
4. Unbeatable / Determined
5. Unwavering / Firm

Look at this list! Imagine you're hiring new salespeople, and see this profile for one of the candidates. Most sales recruiters would hire them on the spot. It looks like an enviable set of silver bullets for sales success. Yet without the right discipline, these bullets backfire.

We found that the root problem lies in the subject area of persuasion. Great salespeople can persuade others because they have first persuaded themselves that their offering holds utility, is of value, and is superior to competitors' solutions. But self-persuasion can be a razor's edge away from self-delusion. Too much self-persuasion can make a salesperson blind and deaf to the customer's actual situation, making them a zealot. Some companies see this and give them the title *evangelist* inside the product marketing department. Other companies don't see it, and leave them in the salesforce.

Customers see through this behaviour in a heartbeat. And when they express doubt, indecision or a contrary view, the Gorilla meets it with a "yes, but" counter-argument as they seek to vanquish the objection and help the customer "get back on track." Whose track is the seller following? Not the buyer's. And that's the problem. Such salespeople aren't really facilitating a mutual discovery, they're manipulating an outcome.

By cross-referencing other areas of The Secret Code, we learned that salespeople who behave this way also have a high fear of failure. They put their head in the sand, don't listen to how the customer answers their questions, and try to close at every opportunity (often prematurely), because they see closing as an attribute of the control and power they crave. Gorillas like to roar and beat their chest.

Of course, the sellers in this group don't recognize they are low-performing any more than the recruiter looking at their behaviour profile sees it. They tend to work longer hours than their peers, make more calls, *deserve* more success, but achieve less. This creates confusion, because it doesn't make sense to them. So, the Gorilla doubles down and makes even more calls, talks even faster, narrates their presentation with even more passion or technical detail to prove their expertise, and gets exasperated if the customer "doesn't get it."

Research undertaken by the University of Bath and Cranfield School of Management provides fascinating insight. Their study published in Harvard Business Review concluded that there are four types of salesperson, and each type uses Gorilla and Guerrilla sales behaviours in different way.[40]:

Twenty-four percent of salespeople are **Masters**. Of these, 100% of them drive next steps, and 84% ask for the sale. Masters are all-rounders who can sell products or value-add solutions equally well. If there is any chink in their armour, it is found in a tendency to assume their value is obvious, and that the customer is as prepared to buy as they are to sell.

Thirty-nine percent of salespeople are **Closers**. 94% of them drive next steps, and 62% ask for the sale. Closers are well suited to commodity products they can present, negotiate and close quickly. They tend to skip needs qualification and go straight to the pitch. Buyers seeking transactional efficiency appreciate their economy. They tend to do well in wholesale or retail roles. But solution buyers just see them as pushy.

Twenty-two percent of salespeople are **Narrators**. 65% of them drive next steps, but only 36% ask for the sale. Narrators sell using demos, catalogues, scripts and canned presentations. They are product experts and technical wizards. If a customer gives an unscripted response or objection, these "talking brochures" see it as a red rag to a bull. They stop listening, lock their horns, and charge at the buyer with all the technical expertise they can muster, to prove their superiority.

Fifteen percent of salespeople are **Socializers**. Only a third of these drive next steps, and only 27% ever ask for the sale. Socializers excel at networking and customer service, but see customers as friends – and feel it's rude to put pressure on their friends. This dynamic can manifest itself in a high cost of sale because they wait for the buyer to take the next step, and *often* give away discounts after an order is received, to sweeten the deal.

It's our observation that the 56% of salespeople matching the Gorilla Journey Motivator for Influence demonstrate a close correlation to the 61% of salespeople who follow the persona loops of Closers and Narrators. The Journey Motivator 'The stronger I am, the more I can influence' permeates the *modus operandi* of both Narrators who bombard buyers with provocative ideas, facts, figures and product mastery, and Closers who use logic or emotion to gain influence.

We also see a connection between the 24% of salespeople who model the persona loop of Masters, and the Journey Motivator of Guerrillas. So, let's examine this group next.

JOURNEY MOTIVATOR 2: 'THE MORE FLEXIBLE I AM, THE MORE I CAN INFLUENCE.' *(GUERRILLA)*

High-performing salespeople believe influence is not about imposing their will on the customer. Achieving a favourable win-win outcome requires adaptability because one approach does not fit all, and every customer is unique. This also means not every customer is the right fit for you as a seller (this is where sales qualification plays a role), and your solution may not be right for every buyer (this is where you tell a customer you're not the best match, but help them find it elsewhere).

Guerrillas can handle this level of adaptation. Gorillas won't, or can't. Letting a customer 'get away' is anathema to them, which is why too often they try to hammer round pegs into square holes.

Iconic Steinway piano salesperson Erica Feidner places round pegs into round holes. She tells us that what she does is not selling, but "matching."

"I memorize the sound, tone, size, make and serial number of every Steinway piano in my inventory," Erica said. "When customers come into one of my stores, I find out about each person, their age, level of experience, how they hold their hand over the keyboard, how they play the notes, their plans to improve at piano or stay at their current level, and what music-in-the-home means to them – is it to be a passing fad or a lifelong gift? This knowledge helps me match the sound that best fits their current or potential life to what each piano can produce. Each piano is different because the timber's timbre is different. I'm able to take them to exactly the right unit every time. But if I don't have the right piano for someone on hand that day, I won't suggest they take second-best based on what I have on the floor. I'll call the warehouse and other stores to secure the right one. If I can't match them, I'll point them to someone who can. That's the discipline needed to sell with integrity."

Erica is indicative of salespeople who don't push their product. They keep a close eye on small but important details, with the intent of placing the customer's long-term satisfaction above their immediate desire to make a sale. That requires enormous confidence and patience. But it builds massive credibility and influence, and in Erica's case, customers for life. When they have a need in the future, or know others who do, hers is the first number they call.

At first glance this looks like a "solution selling" methodology. However, as Dilip Mailvaganam of Microsoft explains, it's actually a way of life. "A key to my success has been building a bank of goodwill with others. You seek opportunities to do things for people, then go the extra mile to exceed their expectations. It's promising something in four days and delivering it in two. It's shutting your laptop when someone talks to you, and giving them your full engagement. It's giving someone a magazine article to read, and instead of just emailing it, you hand-write ideas for them across it (digitally of course). Being there for other people makes them more inclined to be there for you."

The following behaviour traits are consistent across each interview transcript and the corresponding behavioural model for people displaying a high intensity of the Guerrilla Journey Motivator for Influence:

Most frequently observed behaviours
1. Respectful / Empathetic
2. Compassionate / Understanding
3. Persuasive / Convincing
4. Charming / Magnetic
5. Sociable / Humorous

Iconic seller Claire Edmunds's first job was at a local chicken farm in the village where she grew up. "It taught me that I never wanted to work with chickens," she said. "It was an interesting psychological exercise, as I started to appreciate how my body language affected the behaviour of the birds, especially the cockerels, who clearly saw me as competition and would attack if they saw fear! I quickly learned to keep eye contact and move as fast as I could. Later, as I started to explore body language and nonverbal communication in more depth, I was able to reflect on that experience and how our behaviour affects our whole environment, not just the humans in it." Great salespeople respect the customer's needs and views, and they cultivate relationships in the customer's company as well as in their own business so they can deliver value. They care about people. Their intent shines through, and this builds trust and influence.

Colleen Schuller from GSK explains it this way: "If you leverage knowledge the right way, it reveals whose agenda you're serving. This is where the magic happens. You must be seen to serve the customer's agenda in every conversation, presentation and proposal. You talk or write about their world, their needs. This takes courage, because so much of what salespeople have been taught is to pitch their own product, features and benefits. That's transactional. Customers expect it to be more strategic, and this starts by talking about them before you talk about yourself."

"Always look at your interrelations in a way that isn't about you, but is about the other person seeing how you can be helpful to them," suggests one high-performer. "This is particularly true in a professional services space, but also of any job in any industry. If you are helpful to your colleagues, clients, targets, in anyway, and not necessarily looking for something in return, you will be successful. That is why relationship building is such a key part of the sales process. Right from the beginning of my career, I have believed in the multiplier effect. You have to do three things that are favourable to a counterpart before you even have the right to ask for a favour or opportunity to discuss business to some degree. You have to go, two or three times with help, as small as it may be, to those individuals in order to earn the right. And that continues throughout a long-term relationship. Your helpfulness to others is paramount before you can ask for something or expect that the other party will be willing to help you out in some way."

Another approach top sellers are using to build influence with customers is the application of social media. In fact, Chuck Pol, formerly of Vodafone, told us "the whole Trump thing has made me curious – in particular his use of social media!"

Industry observers have noted a decline in the effectiveness of outbound B2B sales calls, when it may take 18 or more phone calls to connect to a new prospect, and only 24% of outbound emails are being opened by the intended recipient. At the same time, 84% of B2B customers now commence their purchasing process via referral,[41] with peer recommendations influencing more than 90% of buying decisions.

This represents a great disconnection of salespeople from buyers. Analysts at Forrester Research[42] believe the disconnect is a backlash against too many sellers having disappointed buyers by being more focused on their own sales agenda and commission cheque than on defining and solving customer problems.

The seminal sales book *Selling to the C-Suite*, based on a 10-year study of executive buying preferences,[43] indicates the internet is more a buying tool than a selling tool. It allows customers to break the "information monopoly" salespeople held in the pre-internet era, and complete much of their own research and comparison online before deciding to meet a salesperson.

Forrester goes on to suggest that by 2020, one million B2B salespeople may lose their jobs to self-service eCommerce, if they rise no higher than the "talking brochure" syndrome described by *SPIN Selling* author Neil Rackham.[44] In these situations the salesperson is more interested in transmitting the contents of a 'figurative' brochure than in creating a meaningful dialogue.

There is evidence to suggest that one answer to the trend of waning outbound call effectiveness is to fight fire with fire by embracing online social selling. This is the strategy of leveraging social media tools to network, prospect and research (in that order) by sharing ideas, opinions and timely content that appeals to your target audience.

This allows sellers to have their personal brand simmer into a following, then boil over into a personal relationship when prospects are finally ready to buy and want to talk to someone they've come to see over time as relevant and credible.

The sniper approach of 'social media selling', where personalized suggestions, eBooks, white papers, blogs, videos and event news are offered to individual prospects, is different from the shotgun approach of 'social media marketing', where the intent is to build awareness of a company or product brand to strangers. Social selling is one-to-one.

Some noteworthy statistics[45] on social media include:

- Seventy-five percent of B2B customers use social media to watch what their peers are doing, and to ask their opinion about buying decisions.
- Fifty-three percent of B2B customers use social media to ask the opinion of others before deciding which supplier to buy from.
- Eighty-two percent of B2B customers say the social content they see associated with a salesperson has a significant impact on their buying decision.
- Seventy-two percent of B2B salespeople using social media outperform their peers, with more than half closing deals as a result.

Jim Keenan, a founder of A Sales Guy Consulting, put it this way: "A lead today can be a complaint on Twitter, a question on LinkedIn or a discussion on a Facebook page."[46]

LinkedIn has found that B2B buyers are five times more likely to engage with people who use social media to provide fresh insights into business or industry.[47]

Social media involves salespeople earlier in the customer's sales cycle, when they are more likely to define the vision for an ideal solution, and by so doing, control the criteria against which other vendors are evaluated.

To be successful in social selling you will need to invest up to four hours each week, going online to monitor the topics under discussion in the chatrooms, LinkedIn forums and slide-share sites. Having done this you will then need to generate your own content if you wish to be noticed by your target audience. Tailor the language of your posts to demonstrate a level of industry-insider expertise.

Remember, social media is a *slow burn* exercise. It may not result in short-term enquiries, but the more your personal brand is seen, the more you'll register as someone to speak with when buyers shift from having a latent need they've learned to live with to feeling an active need they want to talk to someone about.

Seventy-five percent of B2B salespeople who are successful in social media say they took some form of training rather than hack away by trial and error. Areas where professional training can prove helpful include:

- Legislation surrounding social media and data privacy, so it doesn't come across as spamming or stalking.
- How to optimize social media channels like LinkedIn, Twitter, Facebook, Instagram and YouTube.
- How to pilot specific social media software that helps monitor your social footprint and automate the dissemination of your ideas across platforms.
- How to write in sound bites that get your point across quickly in a social media setting, rather than writing lengthy dissertations on product features

and benefits that people switch off from after the first sentence. With social media, less is more.

Smart salespeople meet with selected marketing colleagues on a regular basis to tap into the latest industry issues and shifting customer needs, which helps keep their social media posts relevant. You may even aquire some cool infographics to use in your posts. So, find a friend in your Marketing department and establish a regular time to hear their ideas. Let them talk, and you may be surprised what insights you learn. Common social media rules can be encapsulated as follows:

General rules
- Share posts several times a day, spaced every few hours.
- Respond to incoming posts quickly. Fifty-three percent of users who tweet at a brand expect a response in under 60 minutes.
- Entertain and inform your audience 80% and sell to them 20%.
- Write in "the Royal We" (we, us, our), not first-person (I, me, my).

LinkedIn
- Personalize all connection requests. Say why you're connecting.
- After connecting, send a welcome message.
- Don't join groups and immediately start pitching.
- Mimic the professional tone of any network you join.
- 1–3 hashtags work best.

Twitter
- Don't single out people who follow you for personal messages.
- Don't buy lists of followers.
- Don't saturate your tweets with keywords.
- Don't hijack other companies' hashtags.

Instagram
- Don't ask people to follow you.
- Don't fill people's Instagram feeds. Post less than on Twitter.
- Eleven or more hashtags work best.

Facebook
- Don't Like your own post. You'll look desperate.
- Don't post photos of people without permission.
- Don't tag people or pages that aren't relevant to your post.
- Don't ask people for Likes, Comments or Shares.
- Hashtags decrease engagement. Don't use them.

Google+
- Always mention users' names when commenting on their posts.
- When sharing, add your own comments before posting.
- Use Google+ formatting – bold, italics and strike-through.

Pinterest
- Provide good descriptions for your pins.
- Link to the original source and give credit.
- Don't use images unrelated to your click-through content.
- Don't only pin your own material.
- Hashtags decrease engagement. Don't use them.[48]

———

On the next page is a worksheet for the Destination Belief of Influence. Find a quiet place, contemplate the questions and write down your responses. This will move you further along on the journey of applying The Salesperson's Secret Code. Following that, we provide additional insights about Influence, which were shared by the iconic salespeople interviewed for the research.

MY INFLUENCE REVIEW

Q1. Where could you benefit from having more influence at work or any other sphere of influence you function in?

Q2. How could you increase your influence in the next six months?

Q3. What barriers might you encounter, and how can you overcome them?

Q4. How might you need to adapt your approach to better influence different people's personalities? Plan this by naming specific people.

Q5. When you have undertaken this exercise in Influence, what results will you expect to observe?

ADDITIONAL INFLUENCE INSIGHTS FROM TOP-PERFORMING SALESPEOPLE

1. Have you ever encountered an assertive salesperson and decided not to buy from them, even though you wanted the product? There are many poor sales practices in the marketplace, perpetuated by shallow training providers and tactically minded managers. The problem has its roots in where people started their sales career, and what they think selling looks like. If they began in the time-sensitive, high-volume trades of multi-level marketing, retail or wholesale, the word "influence" may have meant something more akin to coercion, so that's what they train the next generation to do. There's no doubt the sales game was once epitomized by the foot-in-the-door techniques of fast-talking deal-makers – a hangover from the Travelling Salesman who proliferated the American West in the 1870s.[49] These "drummers" of goods and snake-oil peddlers later sold encyclopaedias,[50] cookware[51] and vacuum cleaners.[52] During the industrial revolution, and the technology revolution, they moved on to automobiles in the 1920s, home appliances in the 1950s and typewriters in the 1960s, which evolved into the computers of IBM and the photocopiers of Xerox in the 1980s. IBM and Xerox shrink-wrapped and kick-started the modern sales

training industry, and most products in this field can trace their lineage to these beginnings. Since then, sales training has come a long way in stamping out high-pressure "influence" techniques. Though they still use sequential questioning frameworks to lead buyers into the shearing pen, they also teach that before you attempt to persuade any customer you first need to establish trust and credibility with multiple people, and be genuine. This is the root of all influence.

2. The advent of the internet has made customers infinitely better-informed. Professional buyers are using a ubiquity of data on prices, customer feedback and globalized supply chains to squeeze vendors for better deals. It's never been more important for sellers to tap these same technologies, push their message to individual buyers and prove how they will address the customer's concerns about need, cost, timing, value and risk (in that order). Learn to use online research tools to profile the background and likely needs of your prospects. Learn to apply data calculations to demonstrate how the customer can't lose with your solution, or when their investment will break even and shift into something that saves time and money or makes profit and return on investment (ROI) for them. These approaches will help you become more influential.

3. Customers allow themselves to be influenced by people they like and trust. Showing empathy lays the foundation for building this type of rapport. Smile when you walk in the door. Look your customer in the eye. Use the power of touch – even a handshake increases their

perception of empathy. Listen actively. Maintain eye contact, lean forward as they talk, making noises of affirmation to acknowledge their words and head-tilts to *show* you are listening.[53] Remember the "silent movie" of nonverbal communications often conveys more than the "talkie." If you find it difficult to relate to a buyer, look for a common interest. Bonding with colleagues is why office workers talk about weekend sports, weather or television on Monday mornings – these common experiences serve as a social leveller, identify you as being part of the same tribe and help build empathy. Do the same with your prospects and customers to become more influential.

4. Be authentic and customer-centric. Some office cultures hype salespeople into a narcissistic focus on awards, accolades and other bragging rights. It's great to celebrate your own importance, but when you walk across the threshold of the customer's lobby, you must assume the attitude that doing the right thing by your customer is your number one priority. Develop a genuine curiosity for how their business works, and discuss with people in your own company how your products, services and connections to other parties can be harnessed to make a difference in the customer's business. Take these ideas to them. A good litmus test is to look back at your last client call, email or presentation and count the number of sentences or slides that started by talking about you and your opinions rather than the customer's needs. It's common to see sales presentations weighted 80% on the side of talking about the vendor. Flip that around and see what a difference it

makes to the customer's attitude. When you're talking about yourself, the customer may feel you're the most boring part of their day and keep checking their watch. Let them talk about themselves and it's very likely they will extend the meeting. Remember, it's not your silver tongue that drives the sale – the tongue is merely a rudder to steer the conversation. Your ability to listen is the real engine that takes you places. The more you speak, the more you hear what you *already* know. The more you listen, the more you hear what you *need* to know. Influencers are good listeners.

5. Influencers spend their time, emotion and energy focused on the things they can do something about. They don't waste their reserves fretting over matters outside their control. When they experience obstacles, they step back, break the situation into its component parts, and sort it into four groups: what they can change using their own abilities (self-sufficiency); what they might change through the favour of another (asking for help); what they might do by combining resources with people (partnership); and what can't be changed (force majeure). The first three approaches will solve most problems. Focus on what you can change. Make your influence felt there. You might not be able to stop world hunger, but you *can* buy a sandwich for the next homeless person you pass on the street. You might not be able to win the whole sale today, but you *can* say or do something to nudge it nearer to the finish line. Influencers know that 'yard-by-yard, the sale is hard, but inch-by-inch, the sale's a cinch'.

6. Apply the rule of reciprocity. This is a tenet of social psychology that says people will give something back when you give something of value to them. The waitress who draws a smiley face or leaves some mints with your receipt is more likely to get a tip than one who doesn't. It's the old idea of "You scratch my back and I'll scratch yours." The Chinese call it *guanxi* – an informal system of looking after each other's interests by giving and receiving favours,[54] which stops short of any impropriety. There are many things you can ethically give a customer that holds value to them, such as saving them time, offering useful information, providing additional resources to get things done, helping them look smart in front of superiors or peers, or making introductions to people they want to know. Building reciprocity builds influence.

WHAT'S IN THE MIND?

The psychologist says...

Influence can be defined as the power to have an effect on people or things. In the world of sales, we know that the value of influencing others is self-evident, be it influencing someone to see value in your product, or to open doors, or to win repeat business. The power of influence in sales goes far beyond salesperson and customer. In today's increasingly complex and ambiguous world the ability to influence key stakeholders in our own organization as well as in the customer's, or to hold sway with different interest or lobby groups, is crucial to sales success.

Marketing Psychology professor Robert Cialdini, author of *Influence, The Psychology of Persuasion*, developed a theory of influence based on six key principles:

1. **Reciprocity** – People tend to return a favour when you do something for them and do not necessarily ask for anything in return. A sense of obligation is created. When did you last gift your prospects and customers something of value to them? Some thought-leadership? A day's free consultancy? A new contact from someone in your network? Each of these can create a desire to reciprocate.

2. **Commitment and Consistency** – If people commit to an idea or goal, they are more likely to honour that commitment. The application for salespeople is to find that joint vision of what is to be achieved and to keep the customer on a track of positive reinforcement of that vision.

3. **Social Proof** – People will do things that they see other people are doing. It's why we follow fashion. It's why good salespeople create momentum and share compelling testimonials.

4. **Authority** – People will tend to obey authority figures, even if they are asked to perform unpleasant tasks. The essence of success is to ensure that along with the "instruction" comes a clear pathway to follow. The lesson for managers is to ensure that they do not simply bark out orders, but provide the necessary guiding hand. The lesson for salespeople is that customers will respond to them if they assume an authoritative stance, devoid of arrogance, but which demonstrates solutions that are relevant.

5. **Liking** – People are easily persuaded by those they like. Don't be afraid to smile. Don't be afraid to reveal a bit of vulnerability. It simply shows that you are human… just like them!

6. **Scarcity** – Perceived scarcity will generate demand, as people do not want to miss out. The lesson to salespeople is to know your value, your claim to fame, your unique selling point.[55]

Being influential is not simply about being strong and assertive, persuasive and charming. This is only one element of influence. Managers and salespeople will increase their effectiveness by taking the time to review how they are influencing in every situation and applying specific influencing strategies to customers who will, in turn, be far more responsive.

THE LAST WORD
ON INFLUENCE

A True Story of Two Pals in the Royal Air Force

In the early 1950s two young men, William and Jim, joined the RAF. In those days, all males in the UK over 18 years of age were required to give two years to what was known as National Service. William and Jim became close friends as they worked on various radar installations up and down the UK, often in very remote locations. Jim possessed an intellect of almost genius proportions. William, himself no slouch in the grey-matter department, relied on Jim for many quick calculations in many a high-pressure situation. Jim was also a master at communicating what he and William were doing to the senior ranks. 'Let them know what we are delivering and they will give us the easy life,' was his motto. After National Service they lost touch, but in the ensuing years William reminisced fondly about the things he and Jim had been up to in various far-flung corners of the country, thanks to Jim's ability to influence the 'high-ups.' A knowing smile would appear fleetingly on William's face and, if others noticed his reverie, they were too polite to enquire further.

Fast-forward almost 50 years, to the late 1990s. William was travelling on the motorway towards the north of England and stopped at a service station for fuel and food. As he approached the entrance to the restaurant, William held the door for a gentleman walking in the other direction. As the latter came through the door, the two men looked each other in the eye and instantly recognized each other. Much hand-shaking and back-slapping ensued. "It's so good to see you, Jim!" William exclaimed. "All these years I've been wanting to buy you a drink to say thank you for everything you did to help make my time in National Service so enjoyable." And so, both of their journeys that day took rather longer than they had originally planned.

It all goes to show that good deeds and acts of friendship, especially when nothing is asked for in return, create a sense of obligation that lasts a lifetime. What goes around, comes around.

Destination Belief
Successful salespeople are influential (Influence)

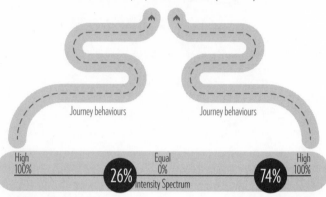

High 100%	Equal 0%	High 100%

26% Intensity Spectrum **74%**

Journey Motivator 1
The stronger I am, the more
I can influence (Gorilla)

Journey Motivator 2
The more flexible I am,
the more I can influence (Guerrilla)

95 percent of low
performers believe
challenge and
assertiveness are the
most effective methods
of gaining influence

92 percent of high
performers focused the
majority their time on
what they are in control
of -attitude, mind-set
and behaviours

87 percent of high
performers acknowledged
what has worked today
might not work tomorrow

At a height of 2,722 feet, the Burj Khalifa, located in Dubai, UAE, is the world's largest artificial structure. The tallest building in the world since 2009, this structure embodies Islamic culture in its design in the form of the spiral minaret. Engineers created this skyscraper to withstand earthquakes ranging from 5.5 to 7.0 on the Richter scale. Rather than remaining rigid, its columns and beams bend, and quake-resisting frames allow positive movement. Acting like shock absorbers in a car, these systems allow the building to flex when it needs to. The building does not assert itself over the earthquake: it is flexible enough to react to its environment on any given day. Translating this example into a sales context, we conclude that achieving an outcome favourable to all requires flexibility because one approach does not fit all; every customer is unique and should be treated so. Rigidity causes sales cycles to break. However, it is hard to accept this if you fear failure intensely. If you do, then letting a customer walk away for the greater good (the long cycle) may be too hard!

84 percent of B2B customers now commence their buying purchasing process via referral

The 56 percent of salespeople matching the Gorilla Journey Motivator for Influence demonstrate a close correlation to the 61 percent of salespeople who follow the persona loops of Closers and Narrators according to HBR research

75 percent of B2B customers use social media to watch what their peers are doing, and to ask their opinion about buying decisions

CHAPTER SIX

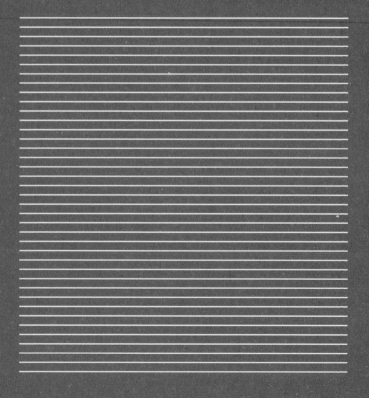

COMMUNICATION

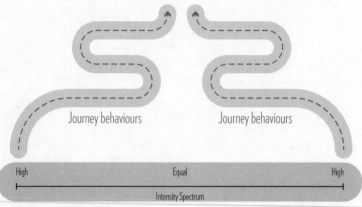

Destination Belief
Successful people know best how to communicate (Communication)

Journey behaviours

Journey behaviours

High | Equal | High

Intensity Spectrum

Journey Motivator 1
Great communication is about
getting your message across
clearly and succinctly (Lightning)

Journey Motivator 2
Great communication is
about developing continuous and
meaningful dialogue (Thunder)

In the 4th century BC, the Greek philosopher Aristotle became a student of Plato, who had been taught by Socrates. Aristotle's views profoundly shaped the next thousand years of Jewish and Christian scholastic tradition, and he was revered among medieval Muslim intellectuals as 'The First Teacher' (Arabic: المعلم الأول). Aristotle was chosen to tutor Alexander the Great, from whom he received an abundance of resources to expand his studies, establish a great library and produce hundreds of books on topics ranging from physics, ethics, theatre and music to politics, biology and zoology.

Aristotle was particularly fascinated by rhetoric – the art of persuasive speaking and writing. He was one of the first documenters of the communication techniques used by actors, merchants and politicians, which he wrote about in the book *On Rhetoric*[56]. In this study, Aristotle identified three elements of persuasive communication – ethos, pathos and logos.

Ethos is Greek for 'character'. It's a method of convincing an audience of your credibility and authority, and therefore the veracity of your proposition. You generate ethos by choosing language appropriate for the audience, employing correct grammar and exuding professionalism. Cite your background and credentials, all the while being knowledgeable and likeable. The purpose of ethos is to build an impression of your authority, competence and credibility. No sales conversation is complete without establishing your ethos. Without it, why should they listen?

Pathos is Greek for 'feeling'. It is used to evoke a stirring emotional connection with what you're discussing. Great speeches and sales pitches build pathos by using light and shade – fast and loud words to convey the excitement of moving forward to achieve one's hopes and dreams (light), and slow whispers or dramatic pauses to drive home why maintaining the status quo is unattractive (shade). The purpose of pathos is to cause the buyer to relate to the beliefs, ideals or product you're offering. No sales conversation is complete without capturing the buyer's heart through pathos. Without it, why should they care?

Logos is Greek for 'reason'. It is used to persuade people by logical thought and facts. This is where you pitch a proposal using data, charts, percentages, case studies and expert testimony, so the audience is persuaded that your reasoning is irrefutable. Logos causes the buyer to feel a logical conviction about what you're selling. No sales conversation is complete without capturing the buyer's mind through logos. Without it, why should they believe?

We might call Aristotle's discovery a 'persuasion chain' that plays out in three acts. Top sellers call these three acts by different names, but the pattern is always the same. One says, 'You sell to the gut, the heart and then the brain – in that order.' Another tells us, 'Before I can sell the logic, I must sell the emotion. To do either, I must sell myself.'

If the templates or sales aids you use to prepare for your sales calls, presentations or negotiations don't remind you to use ethos, pathos and logos, you're missing a key part of the communication process that differentiates the best from the rest.

Our research revealed that all salespeople believe in the power of effective communication. As Louis Jordan put it, "Communication is the primary utensil in the process of selling." Sellers rely on it to learn, to inform, to convince and to follow-up. As with the other four elements of the Secret Code, there exist two Journey Motivators for Communication.

Journey Motivator 1 says great communication is about getting your message across clearly and succinctly – a flash of lightning to illuminate a specific conversation or topic (*Lightning*).

Journey Motivator 2 says great communication requires a more continuous, two-way dialogue – a long rumbling of thunder that bounces between hills and sky (*Thunder*).

The former is a brief, dazzling distraction that strikes, turns heads and then is gone. The latter is ongoing and makes a more permanent impression. It's a concept that mirrors the observation of Pulitzer Prize-winning poet W. H. Auden: "The ear tends to be lazy, craves the familiar and is shocked by the unexpected; the eye, on the other hand, tends to be impatient, craves the novel and is bored by repetition." The ear and the eye. Thunder and lightning. You need both to create a revenue storm. But how much do you need of each?

Destination belief: Successful salespeople know how best to communicate (Communication)

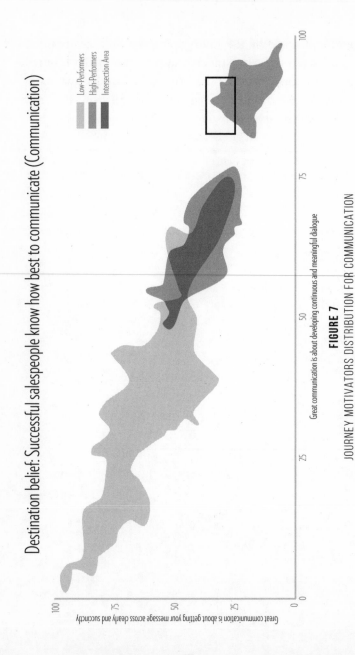

Great communication is about developing continuous and meaningful dialogue

FIGURE 7

JOURNEY MOTIVATORS DISTRIBUTION FOR COMMUNICATION

Great communication is about getting your message across clearly and succinctly

Low-Performers
High-Performers
Intersection Area

You can see in *Figure 7* that the vertical axis shows Journey Motivator 1 (Lightning) and the horizontal axis shows Journey Motivator 2 (Thunder). Note the location of the rectangle where the high-performers cluster. It reveals that top performers believe it's more important to deliver a constant rumble of formal and informal two-way communication to customers (Thunder) than it is to give the occasional pitch-perfect, one-way flash (Lightning). But they *balance* the two, making sure their prospects and customers hear their thunder 79% of the time, with lightning striking 21% of the time. Low-performers tend to operate with a reverse logic.

What does this mean in practical terms? It's quite straightforward. To illustrate, let's explore the Journey Motivators.

JOURNEY MOTIVATOR 1:
'GREAT COMMUNICATION IS ABOUT GETTING YOUR MESSAGE ACROSS CLEARLY AND SUCCINCTLY.' (LIGHTNING)

Just like a lightning strike, the customer feels this type of communication is unpredictable, as it doesn't always arrive as part of an ongoing dialogue. It's where you hit your prospects with a campaign or pitch that arrives 'out of the blue,' in the hope that the offer will electrify them.

Such communication requires preparation. You need to find prospects with something in common. Hone your message with a print or verbal headline that's relevant to their general situation, followed by information that efficiently introduces you (ethos), resonates with them (pathos), and makes sense (logos).

The danger with this approach is that it starts with talking about yourself – and some salespeople don't know when to stop. Those who default to the Lightning approach believe that a good seller is judged by how well they know their product, company history and current affairs in the marketplace. They feel that in educating customers as to why their product is the best, and by giving detailed presentations, the logic of the purchase will be self-evident to the buyer. They cover ethos and logos, yet ignore pathos. In our interviews, we heard this belief coming through in many different guises:

- "It's important to know your product inside-out so as not to get caught out."
- "I sell a complex solution in a crowded market so I need to ensure that customers understand our USP (unique selling proposition)."
- "I have very experienced customers. They want to know that they are dealing with someone who can hold their own."

Not surprisingly, these beliefs came from the lower-performing group.

When we asked the 500 bottom-performing sellers why they thought customers didn't buy from them – even after receiving a seemingly flawless presentation – 61% told us, "I guess I didn't communicate clearly enough." We found that this response behaviour was a strong inclination to fix the situation by following the same formula, and to *try harder* to get their point across. Cue the lightning.

By cross-referencing other pieces of the code, we saw that a majority of this group are the same people who fear failure. This combination makes them communicate by hammering their message even harder, in the hope that turning up the voltage will break down the barriers. Their other reaction is to disengage from the current prospect and repeat the same approach with the next. One seller summed up what we heard from many: "When a customer says 'No' I jump to the next one. But for every 20 who reject me, I'll find one who asks for a brochure, or who agrees to a meeting. That tells me I'm getting somewhere!"

The enthusiasm is commendable, but this pitch-and-run approach is tragic when you examine sales statistics. While it's never acceptable to harass a customer, salespeople *do* need to display a modicum of assertiveness when prospects throw up objections, because an average sales conversation will see the prospect evade commitment eight times before finally agreeing to buy[57]. There's a saying that lightning doesn't strike twice in the same place, and perhaps some salespeople believe they've fulfilled their mission if they try once then move on. But NASA has proved that lightning almost always strikes multiple times in exactly the same place,[58] and so must salespeople.

The following behaviour traits are consistent across each interview transcript and the corresponding behavioural model for people holding the Lightning Journey Motivator for Communication:

Most frequently observed behaviours
1. Unbeatable / Determined
2. Vigorous / Energetic
3. Bold / Courageous
4. Outspoken / Free-speaking
5. Challenging / Assertive

What you see in this group of behaviours is the type of salesperson who will have personal presence, even power. They will challenge and enjoy the fray. They will enjoy the spirited cut and thrust of debate. But if sellers communicate using only ethos and logos, no matter how challenging and charismatic they are, the results will always be less effective than for sellers who use pathos to create, develop and sustain a much more memorable discussion. Where are the empathetic skills here? Where are the listening skills? The ability to be agile and flexible?

Without the emotional content, a sales pitch can only focus on facts and opinions. The types of buyers who respond to this are those who have already had their emotional epiphany, have researched their options, possibly decided on a preference, and are now verifying facts and figures and testing the market to ensure that the vendor they prefer is on par with the available alternatives.

At any given time, only 3% of customers will be actively buying like this – the rest won't be.[59] Seven percent intend to change sometime, 30% see a need but aren't ready to act, 30% see a need but aren't interested in your company, and 30% don't have a need.

In the end, sales behaviour driven by the Lightning Journey Motivator has a limited window of opportunity because it only appeals to a certain type of buyer who may already be near the end of the purchasing process. If your product is simple, commoditized or so easily understood that a customer can complete most of the buying steps without your involvement, then, by definition, the sales process is about marketing to create awareness, and order-taking to complete the transaction. In this environment, salespeople may not be needed at all, especially as digitization takes an increasing hold in our business lives.

Selling Power magazine's CEO Gerhard Gschwandtner once wrote an article titled, 'Are You at Risk of Being Replaced by Technology?'[60] In it, he pointed out how cellphones eventually replaced phone booths; hole-in-the-wall ATM machines replaced bank tellers; automated answering systems replaced switchboard operators; and streaming services replaced video store clerks. He suggested that we are in a 'displacement economy' where technology is driving out old ways of doing business.

Commenting on this, Garth Moulton, co-founder of crowd-sourced data service Jigsaw.com, said he believes technology is helping transfer jobs from face-to-face salespeople to inside teams who sell by Web, email, chat or phone. In the move away from field-based sellers, he expects to see savings in cost and headcount. Jim Dickie, a partner in the research group CSO Insights, said that if all a salesperson can do is talk about the product, their job is certainly at risk. He feels the role of traditional sellers needs to evolve accordingly.

Does this mean that salespeople with the Lightning Journey Motivator are going to dwindle to extinction?

In industries where the product is simple and in demand, and where customers can self-educate before placing an order, the seller's role is almost wholly administrative and centred on processing the paperwork. Profit-seeking financial directors are likely to replace such roles with web-based order fulfilment systems.

However, in industries where the product is highly complex, scientific or customized, the ability to talk matters over with a product-focused expert is likely to remain a key part of the purchasing process. We see that salespeople in the Narrator and Closer persona loops work well in these types of industries because their script revolves around ethos and logos – the person and the product.

Analysts at McKinsey & Company offer this observation:

Gone are the days when the same sales representative could offer all products to all buyers. Salespeople are being required to sell more and more products and solutions as a result of industry consolidation, proliferating products, and more sophisticated buyers. Customers are pressuring their suppliers to bring the full depth of expertise to every sale. As a result, B2B companies must decide between having a number of sales forces to sell different products, or adding layers of sales specialists who can assist colleagues on the front line. As one purchasing manager said, "Most times, the pure sales guy will not help us at all – we really need the technical expertise to design the right solution."

Consider the experience of the networking-equipment group Cisco Systems. Besides helping to deploy virtual-interaction solutions in sectors as diverse as health care, higher education and manufacturing, the company uses 'virtual specialist' support to service its own customers. This change has reduced travel costs for sales specialists by 50% globally, saving millions of dollars a year. It has increased the time sales reps spend with customers by an average of 40% and improved the reps' productivity and home/work life balance. Customers now find that sales specialists are more accessible. Finally, sales reps can spend more time on high-value face-to-face selling activities, such as complex interactions with current clients and efforts to find new ones.[61]

What's clear is that salespeople with these beliefs do well in high-volume transactional sales when they're clear about the function they fulfil. Problems arise when employers incorrectly title them, measure them and train them to play a role different from the reality of the one they really serve – because, for instance, a new sales training concept is in vogue (e.g., styling people as 'solution sellers' when they play a purely product-focused role). Helping staff feel they are fit-for-purpose and not deficient is key to having a productive and motivated workforce. This begins with having different, accurate job descriptions for different sales roles, and aligning measurement and remuneration correctly. As the saying goes, 'Never attempt to teach a pig to sing; it wastes your time and annoys the pig.'

What's also clear is that salespeople with the Lightning Journey Motivator don't prosper where pathos and persuasion are needed in the end-to-end sales process. All told, such sales situations are best handled by salespeople who believe in Thunder.

JOURNEY MOTIVATOR 2:
'GREAT COMMUNICATION IS ABOUT DEVELOPING CONTINUOUS AND MEANINGFUL DIALOGUE.' (THUNDER)

High-performers have continuous, meaningful and adaptive dialogue with their customers because building credentials, even when there's no immediate gain in sight, is the surest way to be in the right place at the right time to spot emerging sales opportunities. Salespeople who do this find themselves in a position to influence the criteria all subsequent suppliers will be assessed against, and thereby gain incremental advantages. They keep their personal and company brands in front of customers and prospects on a regular basis, knowing that repeat exposure and repetition (via email, print, phone calls, texts, meetings and social media posts) is like a peal of thunder in a mountain pass – it reverberates back and forth, up and down, long after the initial conversation.

As one top-performer explained, "My job description is for the customer to regard me as someone they should have in their inner circle when they choose to explore ideas my company provides solutions for. For that to happen, they need to know me, trust me and see that my contributions to them aren't only made when they put money on the table."

The following behaviour traits are consistent across each interview transcript and the corresponding behavioural model for people holding the Thunder Journey Motivator for Communication:

Most frequently observed behaviours
1. Sociable / Companionable
2. Generous / Sharing
3. Challenging
4. Charming / Magnetic
5. Inspiring / Motivating

When we asked the 500 top-performing sellers why they think customers sometimes *don't* buy from them, a majority told us something like, "The message, the audience or the timing was wrong. So, I ask questions, listen hard, and use what I learn to recalibrate." Louis Jordan expressed this sentiment in the following way: "When I was first involved in building commercial relationships, I did not listen hard enough to what the client really wanted. On more than one occasion I cut corners, made assumptions, thought I knew best. This was one of the most valuable lessons I learned in sales. The bullet only needs to be 1mm off so it is critical to be a fanatical observer. That 1mm error will be 1 mile out when it gets to the target. Don't assume you understand; keep going. You have to ultimately make a judgment call, but don't jump to judgement about any given situation too soon."

We see here that the Lightning Journey Motivator inclines sellers to strike harder, while the Thunder sub-belief allows a more contemplative realignment. For example, one high-performer spent ten years working on his single key account and he had no other client during that time. "My firm actually asked me to move to California to work on the account. I started out as the Junior Partner, and spent five years in this role during which time I developed a continuous and meaningful dialogue." Would you be willing to hold your nerve and adopt the Thunder Journey Motivator more intensely than the Lightning Journey Motivator? This partner did, and his reward came at the five-year point. "The account came up for rotation and they had to pick a new Client Lead. I had a significant advantage because of the relationship we had built and, ultimately, they wanted me to become the senior partner. I spent the next five years running the engagement on a global basis based here in LA. Had it not been for those first five formative years, I would not have been offered the position. Whether it is giving consulting advice, sharing articles or making introductions, there are thousands of little things that form the basis of a relationship. These things matter, and you should offer them without expectation of anything coming back the other way in return. That applies to clients and targets, but also colleagues and co-workers."

The Thunder sellers listen to customers far more than the Lightning strikers. This can be hard to do, for it takes a degree of confidence in your own expertise and a willingness to put in the hours for what might look like scant reward. In the end, it comes down to a matter of faith – a belief that this is the right way to grow business. Thunder sellers are much more curious; they ask better questions as a consequence of their enquiring minds and genuine interest in the other party.

Harriet Taylor of Oracle told us: "To be a problem- solver I don't take a tell/sell approach. I use my charisma and social skills to build trust in me as a person long before getting into any sales discussion. I am one of those curious, inquisitive people who asks questions to really understand my customers, their goals and challenges. This is paramount."

Her approach is typical of high-performing salespeople. Curiosity drives them to ask difficult questions – not just to qualify the sale, but to truly put themselves in the customer's shoes. They listen in greater proportion to the time they spend talking, and display an innate respect for the other party, with no presumption that the seller has a monopoly on wisdom.

A top salesperson from Apple shared this: "We have to be students of our customers' businesses, and their customers, their markets and their competitors. The best person to tell us is the customer. So, we listen."

Louis Jordan says this: "I think it is essential to empathize with customers. If you don't care it will bounce back. It is what elevates selling to the next level. That ability, to enthuse another person with how your recommendation will enhance and advantage them, leading to a greater output for them, is paramount. As you progress through your career you of course work with people who are five pages ahead of you in the book, so to say. You learn from them and learn from their experience. One of the keys to being a good communicator is to observe. Listen to the way people frame ideas and communicate the ideas; watch how they use body language and show their ability to listen. When you are listening, you are observing. Everybody who is superb at selling has learned how to do it, sometime, somewhere."

American business book author Keith Rosen has posed the following question to salespeople: "Think about when you were formally trained on how to listen. Chances are you weren't. Very few of us were formally taught effective listening skills. Most of the time we believe listening is simply hearing the words coming out of the client's mouth. Now, if we know that effective listening makes a dramatic difference, why don't we listen better? Well, probably because it takes concentration, hard work, patience, the ability to interpret other people's ideas and recap them, as well as the ability to identify non-verbal communication such as body language. Listening is a very complex process, as well as a learned skill which requires conscious effort, our intellect as well as our emotions."[62]

He suggests there are eight mistakes that limit our ability to listen:

1. Are you thinking about something else while the client is talking? *(**Dreaming**)*

2. During your conversation with a client, do you wait for a pause, so you can spit something out? *(**Answer-preparing**)*

3. How difficult is it for you to stay quiet? Do you say something without thinking first? *(**Compulsive / impulsive**)*

4. Are you faking your listening to the client just so you can get in your comments? *(**Ambushing**)*

5. Do you practise selective listening? Do you only hear the things you want to hear based upon your own prejudices? *(Judging)*

6. Are you unaware of the message the person is sending through body language, such as facial expressions, eye contact and vocal intonation? *(Not fully present)*

7. Do you allow background noise in your environment to hinder your ability to listen? *(Noise-induced stress)*

8. Do you listen through filters, based on a past experience or a similar situation with another client? *(Comparing)*

Keith also offers eight ideas for becoming a better listener:

1. Encourage silence to show you are actively listening. Embrace pauses.

2. Never interrupt while the client is speaking.

3. Be present. Put down your electronic equipment.

4. Make the client feel heard, with such comments as, "What I'm hearing is..." or "Tell me more."

5. Become a solution-oriented listener. Listen for the intended solution more than for the problems.

6. Listen for what is not being said. Find the meaning behind the words.

7. Resist the temptation to rebut. Don't argue.

8. Listen for information you can use.

As the American physician and poet Oliver Wendell Holmes, Sr. (1809-1894) wrote, "It is the province of knowledge to speak and it is the privilege of wisdom to listen."

Top performers are curious about customers as individuals, what drives them, what they're interested in, what they're trying to achieve, why they haven't achieved it already, what's holding them back, what the consequences are if they don't, and how they relate to other people in the organization. They are also curious about how they'd improve the customer's business if they sat on its board. These conversations centre on curiosity and listening.

Louis Jordan told us about the sale that gave him the most satisfaction in his career. "When I first started in a big professional services firm, the largest-size project that had been sold had been about a quarter of a million pounds. I had been asked to go and meet someone relatively junior in an insurance firm. It was soon very clear it was a large opportunity. The person I was speaking to was clearly going to have a rapid rise through the organization. It quickly became apparent to me that there was the chance to create a real relationship. I listened. I empathized. I left that meeting to return to the office and took a call in my taxi telling me we had won the first phase of a project that would lead to a long-term multi-million pound relationship. That was something of a revolution. The person in charge of the project at the client earned the highest bonus two years running, and is a lifelong friend more than twenty years later. He named one of his children after me. Of course, we had very difficult obstacles to overcome, but it was a watershed in both our lives. When I took that call in the taxi to learn we had been taken into the first phase, I couldn't agree it because I wasn't a partner. But I was made a partner shortly thereafter! The line on the graph changed quite dramatically. They wanted someone empathetic."

High-performers believe they should start each discussion in a state of 'unknowing.' Theirs is an empty cup waiting to be filled, not a full cup waiting to be emptied.

It's possible that by openly discussing the goals, barriers and possible resolutions, a seller can close a buyer on the concept alone, and never once get into detail on which products or services they'll use. If asked to get technical, they can go there, but it's not what they open with.

How people's personal goals can be accelerated if the company achieves its business goals is something most customers have already considered before you come along. But since most salespeople only talk about their own product, your voice will sound like a crack of thunder above the din of the crowd when you show you're interested in connecting these dots for them. This is where pathos enters the conversation – by including what's in it for them, you give the customer something very personal to care about. Win their heart. Then win their mind.

Harriet Taylor suggests being mindful that most sales require more than one person to sign off, so it's prudent to join these dots with multiple people. This requires a high level of adaptability because the solution may need to satisfy different people for different reasons.

"You have to gain consensus. Clients want solutions that are ready-made yet also tailored. The key is to not play your hand too early, pitch your product first, and have people tell you it doesn't look like what they had in mind. They can't have your solution in mind until you put it there!" says Harriet. "So, you have to gain insight up front, then link what you hear about them with what you know of current or emerging trends in their industry. Give them a reason to see you as an expert with rare knowledge they should listen to. This disarms any preconceived notions they come with. It empties their cup and puts you in a position to fill it with how they get from where they are today to where they want to be."

Selling like this means regarding pre-built presentations and solutions as guidelines, not fixed standards. The stories and examples told by these salespeople change from contact to contact, and are always tailored to what they first learned should be the key plot points in the story they tell. When the customers hear their own, unique story played back to them, they readily relate, and see themselves as the hero. Research shows that in any presentation, 63% of people remember the stories while only 5% remember the statistics. What story did your last sales presentation tell?

In closing this chapter, we'll share a story that resonates as powerfully today as it did when it happened back in 1978. A top salesperson was trying to close what was the biggest deal of his career to date. In a previous meeting at the customer's site he waited for his appointment in the lunchroom, and chatted at the coffee machine with a supervisor not directly involved in the project.

This employee let slip that all the kids in his son's school had collections of six-inch *Star Wars* action figures, but he hadn't been able to buy his son any because the popular characters had sold out within hours of being released. He couldn't find any Stormtroopers, there was no Obi-Wan Kenobi to be had, and Jawas with a vinyl cape were especially rare. With the shipping procedures of the late 70s, it could take months for such items to restock. This story was a passing reference, small talk, and it meant nothing to the sale.

A few weeks later there was a management reshuffle in the customer company, two departments merged, and the fellow at the coffee machine inherited decision-making responsibility for the deal. Our salesperson heard who the new boss was, and realized he'd met him already. It gave him an idea.

When he went in to make his pitch for the business, he placed a large sheet of paper on the boardroom table, which he had carefully drawn on in black pen the night before. It showed a map of circles, with dotted lines connecting them. They were labelled 'Tatooine', 'Death Star', 'Rebel Base' and 'Trench Run', evoking key locations from the first *Star Wars* movie.

In his briefcase, he had a collection of the coveted Star Wars figures and a blob of Blu-Tack adhesive. He told the story of how the customer organization first woke up to the need for change, who championed the idea, and which staff put time into giving the idea flight. Toy figures of R2-D2, Luke Skywalker and the rare Obi-Wan Kenobi and Jawa characters were affixed to the paper, with the names of real staff written next to them. The issues they were dealing with were jotted onto the paper in a different-coloured pen.

The story told how they had a destination in mind, but first had to blast through uncertainties and challenges in the Death Star. This circle began to fill with half a dozen Stormtroopers, each of which had a blank cardboard tag taped to its head. The salesperson insisted the stakeholders in the room decide which six needs were their most important priorities, and these were written onto the tags.

After a trip through hyperspace with Han Solo at the helm, the heroes arrived at the Rebel Base, and the vendor's solution was explained. How the vendor would implement that solution was written in the Trench Run circle.

The audience then debated whether each element of the vendor's solution had the power to shoot down the Stormtroopers still standing on the page. Half the fun was agreeing how the solution needed to be tweaked, and then toppling the Stormtroopers with a slash of Obi-Wan's plastic light-sabre and Chewbacca's crossbow.

The seller asked each person how achieving those outcomes would feel, and he wrote this down next to their names. He then drew a red explosion over the Death Star, a set of numbers, and in large capital letters wrote 'MISSION ACCOMPLISHED.'

When the executive in charge asked if they would be receiving a formal proposal, the seller pointed at the colourful schematic and said: "This is what we will do together (pointing at the Rebel Base). These are the problems it will solve (Stormtroopers) and how doing so will make you all feel. Here is what it will cost (the numbers next to the Death Star explosion). You know where to find me, and I'd like you to keep the toys. May the Force be with you." With that he packed up his briefcase and left the room.

His last impression was seeing the executive's face change as the realization dawned on him that the seller had remembered their coffee conversation from weeks earlier, had gone to the trouble of seeking out the hard-to-find action figures, and had tailored a fun presentation that not only answered their questions as a company, but also his need as a father.

The salesperson had pitched the most expensive solution, and won with ease. People still recalled the innovative presentation years later – the salesperson's thunder rumbling long after the competition's lightning had flashed and been forgotten.

———

On the next page is a worksheet for the Destination Belief of Communication. Find a quiet place, contemplate the questions, and write down your responses. Doing so will move you further along on the journey of applying the Salesperson's Secret Code. Following that, we provide additional insights about Communication, which were shared by the iconic salespeople interviewed for the research.

MY COMMUNICATION REVIEW

Q1. Which of the 8 factors potentially limit my ability to truly listen to my customers? In what ways will I be different going forward?

Q2. Do customers hear from you like a sudden lightning strike, or like the rolling thunder? What do you want to keep the same, or change? (Think about this in the context of the balance of logos, ethos and pathos.)

Q3. Are you curious enough about your customers? What will you do differently to demonstrate an interest in them?

ADDITIONAL COMMUNICATION INSIGHTS FROM TOP-PERFORMING SALESPEOPLE

1. See every stakeholder as unique. Plan how you will communicate to show that you see them as more than just another number. Take care to prepare before each contact. Frame your questions so they will see they are designed uniquely for them by including references to things they previously told you (or use ideas you see they have posted online). Explain how your value proposition advances their personal or corporate goals, and ask if it's an outcome they want, and what achieving that will mean to them or their team.

2. Create memorable experiences by doing something no other salespeople do. Poet and civil rights activist Maya Angelou said, "People will forget what you said, people will forget what you did, but people will never forget how you made them feel." Treat them with respect. Remember small courtesies. Invite them to meet you at venues they wouldn't normally have access to. When you're in the discovery stage of the sale, invite them to meet you at dawn for a hot-air balloon ride, and theme your questions with reference to 'a bird's eye view', 'staying aloft', 'the next level' and 'horizons.' When you reach the presentation stage of the sale, take them to a racetrack, let them

rev a powerful engine, and gear your pitch towards speed, control and acceleration. Print wads of play money in large denominations, put it in a briefcase, and ask the customer to open the case in the middle of a meeting and tip out the contents. Explain that the pile of money they shake out is equal to the ROI your solution will deliver in the first year. Arrange to introduce them to businesspeople you know they admire. Send a book to their favourite author to get signed and personalized, then present it to them as a thank-you note. Print a picture of a bull with dotted lines to show all the cuts of beef; label each butcher's cut as a problem your solution will eliminate. If they eventually buy from you, take them out for an expensive dinner to mark their graduation from 'steakholder to stakeholder'. (If they buy from someone else, send them a set of steak knives as a consolation prize.) Creative salespeople know how to communicate in memorable ways. And while some of those ideas might seem completely crazy, they were all provided by top-performers during our interviews. If you found yourself thinking, "That will never work," you may wish to explore why you hold that limiting belief. What might it be like if it *did* work?

3. The best communicators demonstrate authentic empathy. They move beyond the rote, "I know how you feel", and respond with deeper content that reveals they've walked in the customer's shoes and can truly relate, using a tone, pace and volume that matches the mood of the buyer. If they don't have any relatable experience to draw from, they ask: "What is that like for you?", "How does this impact on you?", "How else?" And they use it as an opportunity to learn.

4. The best sellers dig beneath the surface of what a customer wants and ask why they want it, why now, what's changed to make it relevant, how do they do it today, what do they like about it, what do they want to change, who has been shouting for change the loudest, who doesn't want things to change, what is everyone's experience making a change of this nature, will it be easy or difficult, what are the risks attached, are there consequences for inaction, is there payback for taking action, when will the window of opportunity close, what will success look like, how will they know when they've found the right solution, what criteria are they using, who wrote them, who influenced their ideas? This is a small sample of questions the iconic sellers told us they use to smooth the communication process.

5. Give positive feedback on things you observe. Catch the customer doing something you admire, and tell them you admire it. It might be the way they facilitated a meeting, or a question that really made you think, or the quality of a presentation they gave, or a charity their department is sponsoring. Some companies have cultures where leaders never give positive feedback. A kind word of recognition for a job well done can stand out like a rich oasis in a parched desert.

6. Stop using slides as a default presentation tool. Your marketing team might like to control format and content, but customers crave discussion, not narration. You will be perceived as more passionate, sophisticated, creative and attentive if you work with paper and pen, tablet and stylus, or marker and whiteboard.

WHAT'S IN THE MIND?

The psychologist says...

We all communicate through various channels every day, yet the power of effective communication is often overlooked. The author S. F. Scudder, in his theory of communication (1980), stated that "all living beings existing on the planet communicate, although the way of communication is different." Think about it. As humans we default to speech, but animals use noises and movements, children cry before they can talk and plants exhibit visible changes to signal their need to be watered. Within this framework, when communication is viewed from a psychological perspective, one must consider not only the flow of information from one person to another, but also the underlying thoughts, feelings, perspectives and reactions.

For salespeople, there is a need to consider the person with whom you're communicating and how you may adapt the communication to suit them. Do they like detail and descriptions or just facts? Short or long emails? Do they prefer to speak on the phone? Do they like to have a personal chat before getting down to business? These are considerations to think about when communicating with a client, stakeholder or peer. Sometimes a simple question such as "How should I contact you?" can establish how the other person likes to be communicated with from a practical perspective. Does the customer prefer email, phone call, text, social media, etc.? Most importantly, make sure whatever form your communication takes is clear and precise. Clarity is important to avoid any mixed messages and to ensure you have the greatest influence on your desired outcome, whether it be closing the deal, negotiating costs or providing insight and value.

THE LAST WORD ON COMMUNICATION

The Moment George H. W. Bush Lost the Presidency of the United States

In one of the final televised presidential debates of 1991, the incumbent, George H. W. Bush, was answering questions on the state of the American economy. The moderator invited one lady in the audience to ask her question and she prefaced it with some personal observations. She spoke about her town, where people were losing their jobs. She spoke about her own family, some of whom found themselves without employment and with little prospect of gaining any. She spoke about the hardship and misery this state of affairs was causing.

The TV cameras cut to President Bush just in time to see him glancing at his watch. He composed himself and proceeded to sympathize with the questioner. He spoke of 'global economic forces.' He spoke of 'macro-economic policy.' He spoke of 'government policy.' He was eloquent, knowledgeable and assertive. He was Presidential.

His debate adversary, candidate Bill Clinton, was invited to comment. He stepped forward towards the lady. He said that he felt her pain. He, too, had friends who had lost their jobs. He recognized the kind of town she was from because that's the kind of town he was from. He was empathetic, measured and spoke in easy-to-understand language. He was human.

The studio audience knew what had just occurred. The audience watching at home experienced the same reaction. Shortly thereafter, Bill Clinton was elected the 42nd President of the United States.

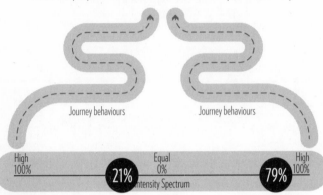

Destination Belief
Successful people know best how to communicate (Communication)

Journey behaviours   Journey behaviours

High
100%   Equal
0%   High
100%

21%   **79%**

Intensity Spectrum

Journey Motivator 1
Great communication is about getting your message across clearly and succinctly (Lightning)

Journey Motivator 2
Great communication is about developing continuous and meaningful dialogue (Thunder)

57% of respondents hold the first sub belief more intensely than the second

43% of respondents hold the second sub belief more intensely than the first

61% of respondents indicated that even when customers did not respond positively to a particular sales message it must be due to that fact that they, the salesperson, had not communicated clearly enough

AC current is reversible, while DC only flows in one direction. AC transfers current over long distances and provides more energy, while DC can only transfer limited energy. For this reason AC power is preferred in homes and industries, while DC is more preferred on electrical devices that are powered by batteries. The problem, of course, with batteries is that, slowly but surely, they run out of power. They grow weak. They must either be replaced or recharged. If you communicate by simply transmitting a message, without stopping to check if it is being received then you will simply be like those discharged batteries. Successful communication, like AC, needs to flow both ways. In doing so it creates continuous and meaningful dialogue over long distances which provides more energy!

43% of respondents recognize that building relationships is more important than making a transaction (because developing long term relationships will help them to be better than they ever thought they could be)

100% of high performers listen in greater proportion to the time they spend talking

100% of high performers are curious about the profession of selling. They are curious about their own performance and how to improve. They are constantly learning, adapting, changing

CHAPTER
SEVEN

UNLOCKING YOUR CODE

In the previous chapters we explored five Destination Beliefs and ten sub- or Journey Motivators. We discovered that salespeople hold both Journey Motivators, and that the secret of the top-performers is that they hold a *specific combination of intensity of each Journey Motivator*. Let's remind ourselves of the optimal balance of Journey Motivators, as illustrated below:

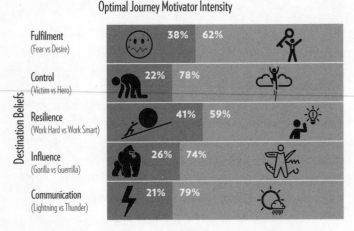

Optimal Journey Motivator Intensity

FIGURE 8
THE 5 DESTINATION BELIEFS & OPTIMAL JOURNEY MOTIVATOR INTENSITY

Your own balance of intensity may align closely to this, or it may be somewhat different. The delta between your current motivation balance and the optimum motivation balance, as demonstrated by the top 5%, represents the size of the shift in your beliefs and motivations which may be necessary if you want to align with the best-of-the-best. As things stand you may be able to draw some conclusions about your own personal 'Secret Code delta'. Having read this far it is reasonable to assume that you have found this book provocative and worthy of reflection. The rest of this chapter is aimed at helping you to shift some of your current beliefs and motivations and to enable you to model (copy) other people who you think display the attributes you would like to own for yourself.

What you will not have at this point is a specific measurement of your 'Secret Code delta'; and so the Salesperson's Secret Code authors have developed a psychometric instrument which provides precisely that. More information can be found at www.salespersons-secret-code.com. Armed with an accurate measurement of the balance of your own Journey Motivators you will have, in sharp focus, a road-map to guide you along the journey towards your destination.

Become a 'Modeller'

Our top-performers have now become our role models. We know that the top 5% succeed in large measure because their beliefs drive them to think and act in ways that support the intensity of their motivation. The iconic salespeople we highlighted throughout this book have provided wonderful examples of how they apply the beliefs to give themselves that special combination that supports their collective success. They have discovered for themselves the right amount of 'tension' between the two Journey Motivators, within each Destination Belief, that enables them to perform at the top of their game.

You may be thinking, "That's all very well for them. They've cracked the code, but how do I do that?" One stratagem is simple: to make the decision to learn from our role models and apply some of their techniques for

> *"By appreciation, we make excellence in others our own property."*

Voltaire,
1694-1778

ourselves. Many great thinkers and creators have found that the best ideas are ones that are 'stolen and improved.' Feel free to *steal* as many ideas as you wish from what you have read here. Just imagine the improvement in sales performance globally if every salesperson everywhere adopted just one or two of the ideas we've learned about and moved their balance of intensity closer to what we now know is the 'sweet-spot' position. Think of it like tuning an old-fashioned radio, before the days of digital streaming. You hear the white noise, and as you turn the tuning dial you hear the faint sounds of the channel you seek. You keep turning the dial and suddenly, there it is − a clear, strong signal. This is very much the same. It may take time, as you turn your inner dial, to find your own clear, strong signal. But it's there, transmitting. Your favourite spot on the dial awaits!

When we adopt some of the behaviours other people display we call it 'modelling'. Anyone reading this book can model. We know this because throughout your life you will have been modelling other people, knowingly or subconsciously. It's how we learn and grow. You will have modelled your parents and may still do so; you will have learned from your teachers; you will have picked up on how to perform tasks from colleagues at work. The list of people you will have modelled in your life is sure to be considerable. As Stephen Sondheim wrote in the musical *Into the Woods*, "Careful the things you say, children will listen. Careful the things you do, children will learn."

Each of us has the capacity to show curiosity about someone or something. We can all pause to watch and listen to how other people operate. All we are inviting you to do is to make modelling something that you do quite deliberately, with full awareness. You can add this information to what you learn about yourself as you live your daily life.

How to Model in 6 Steps

1. Focus on one specific aspect of what you observe in someone that you want to acquire for yourself. For example, you may want to become a Guerrilla and less of a Gorilla (see Chapter 5: Influence) and have admired how a colleague seems to have influence over others. That's a skill you want to emulate. Identify the effect their behaviour or talent has on you and others. What do you see, hear and feel? When you have done this, you have found the 'Wow!' factor. Step 1 is about 'What' and 'Who' and 'Wow!'.

2. Watch them: watch them work; watch them talking to other people and the effect their behaviours have; watch the way they move, perhaps with confidence, head held high. You may discover that, as they are doing this, other people seem to gain confidence. Step 2 is about watching the 'How'.

3. Ask them: invite them to imagine themselves using the talent you have observed and gain their insights. Be very clear that they may take some time to uncover those insights because they may not be aware of the talents you have observed. Frame your questions in the present tense, and ask your model to describe the following relative to the performance of a task:

a. What is around you?
b. What are you doing?
c. What are you saying?
d. What talents are you using?
e. What truly matters to you in this moment?
f. How would you describe yourself?

Let's build on the example from steps 1 and 2. You may ask your model, "As you're walking into your meeting with your head held high, how would you describe yourself?" Let's assume the reply is something like, "I am a subject matter expert who is sure-footed. I am someone who will listen to my customer's concerns and respond in ways that show I am in tune with their situation. I will encourage them to view me as their ally." In that moment, you may have discovered something that you can use, something that can enable you to be a little different. They have described *Guerrilla* attributes. How might you have answered if asked the same question? Would you have described *Gorilla* attributes in observing your own behaviour? In this moment, you may have identified a way to 'tune your own dial. Step 3 is about 'Ask'.

4. Reflect upon what you have learned from your observations and your conversations. Then, step into your model's shoes, leaving behind any preconceptions you may hold. Just assume that what they say and do is now the way *you* say and do. And be it! Step 4 is about 'Do'.

5. As you adopt the behaviours of your model, see what aspects of what you are doing make a difference to you. Be prepared to discard something if it patently is not helping to produce an improvement for you. Be 'fully present' and aware as you are modelling the new behaviour. Step 5 is about 'Evaluate'.

6. Make a note of the process, behaviour, language pattern – whatever it is that you have modelled. Allow it to be absorbed into who you are. Allow it to become your identity. This can take time – give it the time required.[63] Finally, Step 6 is about 'Adapt and Adopt.'

Below is a summary of the six steps.

FIGURE 9
THE 6 STEPS TO SUCCESSFUL MODELLING

Today, we live in what has been called a VUCA world – volatile, uncertain, complex and ambiguous. Old certainties are no longer quite so certain. The pace of technological advancement and the impact of globalization are having unforeseen, often disorienting effects. The ultimate consequences are unfathomable. Now, more than ever, the requirement to keep learning and developing is obvious if we are to successfully navigate the way ahead. The choice to model – or not – is yours.

Play with What You Believe

This study has been about beliefs. The beliefs held by our top-performing salespeople drive them to behave in certain ways; those behaviours lead to specific outcomes. But what exactly *is* a belief, and why is it so vital to understand what we believe and why?

Let's start with a statement: 'If I don't wear a scarf during cold winter weather I will catch a cold.'

Is this true? Is it untrue? What were you taught by your parents when you were a child? It will, of course, depend largely upon where on planet Earth you were brought up, but we can all agree this point: the possible outcome of catching a cold if I don't wear a scarf may, or may not, happen. If it does happen, then perhaps the statement is true. If it does not happen, maybe I just didn't catch a cold this time, but next time I will. I may still hold on to the belief that not wearing a scarf in cold weather is a risky business.

You can easily observe that the statement about cold weather, scarves and illness has nothing to do with fact, nothing to do with accuracy and *everything* to do with faith, a blind certainty, and an emotionally held truth. It is a belief. You may laugh at the hypothesis that failing to wear a scarf means that catching a cold is inevitable – as night follows day, if I forget my scarf between November and March, I will become ill. "*Preposterous!*" you may cry. But the plain fact is, you either believe it or you don't.

Beliefs are emotionally held opinions that we assume to be fact.[64] Beliefs provide us with the motivation to deploy certain talents or skills. They may promote or inhibit certain behaviours. And they have a major impact upon our sense of self, of who we are, and why we do what we do.

This is why we can observe such marked differences in the low- and top-performers. This is why we can readily see why our Iconics have succeeded as they have.

What we often hold to be true, both for ourselves and others, are presuppositions. We presuppose their veracity, act in ways that support the presupposition and reinforce the same presupposition as a belief when we 'discover' it worked or fulfilled its promise. And beliefs have been at the root of some of humankind's worst excesses (the Holocaust, the Inquisition, Apartheid, etc.) and better moments (the founding of the United Nations, the day Yuri Gagarin became the first space traveller, or Bob Geldof's unshakeable belief that music could help eradicate Ethiopian famine). As we believe, so we will behave. Beliefs are at our very core.

We have, therefore, been inviting you to think about how your beliefs affect the salesperson, sales leader or human being you wish to be. But how do we begin to change previously held presuppositions about ourselves and the world we inhabit? Let's return to our scarf and the cold winter's day. How do I 'let go' of my belief that the scarf is essential to my good health? Well, imagine what it might be like if I were to dare to go outside on a cold day without a scarf. I may feel the cold air on my neck and quite like it. I may appreciate that I feel less restricted with no scarf wrapped tightly around me. I may suddenly notice that many other people in the street are also walking around looking perfectly healthy and not wearing a scarf. That is the 'Law of Similarity' – we notice those who are like us and want to be like them. In short, to begin to shift a belief, I can tentatively 'try on' another belief. If it really causes me pain and anguish I can always go back to wearing

my scarf. The trick is to dare to try! What's stopping me?
Might I be afraid that I may prefer a scarf-less existence?

Trying On New Beliefs

1. Choose one of the Journey Motivators that you would
   like to move towards as a way to rebalance the intensity with which you hold each Journey Motivator. Think
   back to the Fulfilment Destination Belief from Chapter
   2. Which Journey Motivator do you want to address?
   You can decide to explore Journey Motivator 1 and
   move towards being free of fear ('I see failure as an opportunity to learn.'). Or ,you can decide to try on Journey Motivator 2 ('I am going to surprise myself and be
   brilliant.') Let's assume you select Journey Motivator 2
   to try on. What would that be like? What is happening
   as you surprise yourself? Maybe you've landed a new
   customer whom you never imagined you would win.
   Maybe you have doubled your annual sales target. Maybe you have hit your numbers in a really challenging
   market environment. What is it that would make the
   difference you want to see and experience for yourself?

2. Now, think of a different situation, a time when you
   were brilliant. What was that like? Where were you?
   What was happening? What were you doing that was
   so remarkable? What were others around you seeing,
   hearing and feeling as they experienced your brilliance?
   We call this process 'association'. You are associating
   with a time when you demonstrated the very attributes,
   skills, talents and behaviours that you are seeking to re-
   capture now. Isn't it interesting that we discover that we
   can already do and be what we think we are missing?

3. As you continue to connect or associate with that time when you were being brilliant you can help yourself to hold the feeling. We call this 'anchoring'. You might touch your wedding ring or your watch as you associate with the feelings, or you might close your eyes. Sometimes, as you anchor, the feelings might dissipate. This is normal, so stop the anchoring process, pause and re-associate in a moment or two. Sometimes it can take several 'trying-on sessions' to anchor successfully.

4. When you are happy that you are associating fully with the time when you were being brilliant, when you *believe* that you are brilliant, reconnect with Journey Motivator 2. Now allow yourself to explore:
   a. Your environment – where you are and what it is like.
   b. How you are behaving – what you are saying and doing that shows clearly that you are being brilliant or surprising yourself.
   c. What talents you are displaying in this moment?
   d. What is important to you and how knowing this is supporting your behaviours and talents.
   e. How being like this affects your appreciation of yourself. What is shifting, moving, evolving?
   f. What wider impact you are now having? Perhaps as you are being brilliant you are becoming a role model for others, or maybe you are setting the tone for how business can be conducted across your industry.

It is important to keep repeating this process – this is how we adopt a cycle of continuous learning and growth. Over time, often imperceptibly, our beliefs about ourselves change. As our beliefs alter, so do our behaviours. We become the embodiment of our new beliefs. In the end, this happens because we have given ourselves permission to be different.

It was Sir Winston Churchill who said, "To improve is to change. To be perfect is to change often." We may not ever be perfect, but we can believe that it's good to try. If we hold this belief, we are prepared to accept that the way we have done things in the past may not be what leads us to future success. We are also accepting the premise that change is good. Who knows, we might even become better than we ever thought possible. As Albert Einstein said, "It's only failure if you stop trying."

CHAPTER
EIGHT

THE SECRET CODE – LESSONS IN MANAGEMENT & LEADERSHIP

Our sales profession has become adept at developing the processes that support sales-customer relationship management systems, key account management processes, strategic relationship mapping and sheets of many and varied colours. Many of these are excellent; tools that no self-respecting professional would be without. It has also become an accepted norm that those of us who make sales our career will be offered sales skills development – how to prospect, how to ask questions, how to frame a proposition and how to demonstrate the value we bring. Again, all perfectly right and proper. No customer should experience a salesperson who is not up to the job. From the sales leader's perspective, we now have a third element to consider. In addition to traditional focus upon processes and skills we now have a more detailed understanding of how deeply-held beliefs will manifest themselves behaviourally. 'Sales transformation' is an epithet which is part of the management lexicon these days. It would be high-risk to implement any process or skills changes without first understanding that the Secret Code exists and then seeking to compare the salesforce with the role-model 5%. Failure to do so would be like driving a car, blindfolded and steering aimlessly towards a destination that you don't know even exists and which you would not recognise, even if you made there in one piece! Sales managers and leaders are now able to focus on their role, knowing how they can have a major impact upon their people's success and their customers' experience of their company. Three areas to consider are:

1. What is the Salesperson's Secret Code? Why and how might it be important and make a difference to me and my team (we have begun to answer that question in this book)?

2. What is the distance between my team's individual motivation balance and the optimum motivation balance demonstrated by the top 5% (the Salesperson's Secret Code psychometric can help. For more information visit www.salespersons-secret-code.com)?

3. In the light of insights provided by the psychometric, what adjustments will each salesperson make to their beliefs and behaviours which will have the effect of changing the 'direction of travel' they are on currently. How can I influence this and what help might I need from both internal stakeholders and external thought-leaders?

The Salesperson's Secret Code is, therefore, a wellspring of insight that explains for the first time why nothing – not strong branding, product advantage, keen pricing, inspirational training, transformative coaching or ingenious sales methodologies – can propel a salesperson to greatness if they don't believe certain things about themselves, about their customers or about selling in general. Any sales manager and leader reading this book will be able to cite examples of salespeople in their company who are consistently successful; and yet in the same instant those same managers and leaders will be able to think of salespeople who are selling the same product or service and have similar skill levels, but who just don't seem to have the same belief, either in themselves or their offering. And as we believe, so we tend to behave. Despite the same opportunity, the consequential results can differ wildly.

This phenomenon is not peculiar to sales. It is seen in many other aspects of the human condition. As the authors are finalizing the manuscript of this book a sporting example looms large in the world of soccer. In the 2015-16 season, Leicester City football club confounded odds of 5,000:1 and won the English Premier League title. This was a club which was nearly relegated the season before, but which took the league title with 81 points, a margin of ten points over the second-placed team, Arsenal. And yet, only nine months later, the same team languishes in the relegation zone, cannot score goals and is rapidly running out of road. The trapdoor out of the Premier League is beginning to open wide. By the time you are reading this, you will know how Leicester City's 2016-17 season ended (or you can 'Google' it) but real the point here is this: given such a catastrophic change in fortune, had the players (and indeed the manager) suddenly become less skilled at playing soccer? Unlikely. Had the rules of the game changed? No. Had all the other clubs in the league improved so much in the off-season that they left Leicester City far behind? Maybe a few had, but surely not all.

Perhaps the truth is far simpler. No one had expected much of Leicester City in the season of its greatest triumph. In the following season, however, the weight of expectation was heavy. Perhaps the players, liberated to be better than they ever thought they could be in their great season, were afraid of failure to a degree, which left them petrified the next. Perhaps, rather than capitalizing on the way they had seized their sporting destiny in 2015-16, the team allowed a run of bad form to become a self-fulfilling prophesy the following year. Normal service had been resumed; perhaps they were a flash in the pan after all – and maybe the players believed it.

Our beliefs about ourselves help to define who we are. When our beliefs are shaken, or challenged, if they are ill-thought through or even absent, then we can wobble.

Let's bring this back to the world of sales. We recall a client whose sales force we were coaching while writing this book. A salesperson we will call Paul was languishing in the bottom 20% of his company's league table. He was affable, looked on the bright side of life, worked long hours and knew his company's product details back to front. We made recordings of his customer sales conversations, and analysts listened to these to track patterns in what he always did well, what he habitually forgot or didn't have the courage to do, and where his skills were hit-and-miss (strong one day but absent the next).

Over several months of coaching, Paul's skills quotient started to fill out and his sales persona loop began to change. He stopped jumping into the product information so quickly. He learned to let the customer speak, to listen and paraphrase. He started quantifying his customer's needs in terms of risk and value. His confidence climbed and so did his position on the league table. For the first half of the financial year he dominated the top position – by all appearances a successful turnaround.

Then Paul lost his grandmother. He took it hard, and needed to take extended vacation as he worked through his grieving process. When he returned to work several months later, his outlook had changed.

Loss and fear now consumed him; he had sunk into a funk that drained his emotional *Resilience* and stunted his *Communication* with customers and colleagues. Compared with losing a family member, workplace concerns now seemed shallow and unimportant. He started turning up late to meetings, or not at all, steadily spiralling out of *Control*. Any political capital or *Influence* he'd earned from his previous ascent now waxed cold.

Paul had the skills to be the best in the business. He'd proven that already. His company's products, lead generation and pricing hadn't changed, and his industry was even experiencing modest growth. He still had the support of a personal sales coach, product trainers, a caring manager and a concerned HR department willing to do whatever was needed to lift him up. Yet he languished, despite having attained *Fulfilment* earlier in the year. He had every reason to succeed, yet his batteries were drained and his belief system was broken.

Paul later pulled out of his nosedive, aligned his beliefs with what you've read as The Salesperson's Secret Code, and is now pacing himself in the top 25% of his company. His story is provided to underscore the fact that beliefs matter. They're the bedrock upon which all else is built.

What does this tell us about the role of sales managers and sales leaders in respect of unlocking the code? In the first instance, the role of managers and leaders in creating the right environment for their salespeople to succeed becomes even more evident. In defining the secret code, based upon our interviews with the top performers, at no point did any salesperson comment negatively about the culture of management in which they operated. Every top performer spoke about knowing what was expected of them, how they were expected to behave, the processes they had to follow and the systems that were in place. To them, all this was a given, a 'hygiene factor'. There are best practice lessons here for managers and leaders. Creating the environment which is most conducive to your salespeople's success is directly connected to assisting arrival at the Destination Beliefs and the optimal intensity of Journey Motivators. Let's explore that now:

Take the Fulfilment Destination Belief. If a manager creates an environment of command and control, of admonishing people every time they step out of line, or telling people instead of asking questions and engaging with them, then we have the perfect environment for driving people towards an intensity biased in favour of a fear of failure. Yes, it may drive people to hit their sales targets, but, as we have seen from our top-performers, they will fail to engage with the behaviours which come from holding the belief that 'I can be better than I ever thought possible'. In the end it may become self-destructive and it certainly smacks of short-termism. It's unsustainable.

As long as your corporate values and procedures are preserved, encourage experimentation and risk-taking. Show your people that you believe in them. Don't penalize mistakes, but encourage each one as something the team can learn from. *There is no failure, only feedback.* This is a belief, not the truth; but if managers can behave as if it were true, then they assist their people along that Journey Motivator of never being afraid to be better than they ever thought possible.

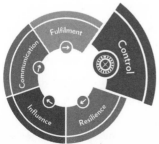

Someone or something must always be accountable for success. This is the Control Destination Belief. Quite clearly, any sales manager or leader worth their pay cheque will seek to create an environment and expect behaviours where each person believes that they are accountable for their success (hero). Of course, there will be times when all of us face moments of misery, when we want to blame anyone and anything for our current state except ourselves. Sometimes events are beyond our control, but when we enable our people to feel that they can turn worries and concerns into positive action and to recognize that, in the end, the buck stops with them, this is when we leave our mark as manager and leader. In your next sales meeting, invite team members to recall their positive sales experiences. Invite them to explain what challenges they overcame, how they did it, and what success felt like, so that they can recall and share these positive emotions. As you do this, remind your people that they are focusing on what they can control and what they can influence. It is easy to get drawn into dialogue about factors that are outside of our control. These conversations sap energy, are infectious and fester; so, as the leader, create an agreed set of standards where these conversations don't take place. The power of recalling past success increases the likelihood of repeated success and will lessen the likelihood of people adopting victim mind-sets.

Take people out of their comfort zones by inviting them to chair a sales meeting or complete a pipeline review. Assign salespeople to interview each other's lapsed customers to find out why they stopped buying or changed suppliers. Have your most experienced team members mentor newcomers. Take their previous personal best and challenge them to better it. In undertaking these and other 'discomfort zone' activities you send a message that your expectation is that there is a solution to every challenge or problem we face and that we have within us all the resources we need to rise to those challenges. 'Action dispels fear' is a management maxim that really can enable people to move away from victim towards hero mind-set.

In creating the right climate for heroes to thrive, it's important to focus on positive perspectives. As the leader, it is important to keep your team focused on positive dialogue and sometimes to the complete exclusion of the balanced view. What went well on the call? What else? What else? (park the 'What could have gone better?' question). A powerful exercise for a group of salespeople is to ask them to write down seven things that they achieved yesterday. You will notice that some find it easy and some will have a blank piece of paper. You now know who in the team you should work with to build their sense of achievement and, therefore, their ability to control their own destiny.

As a manager and leader, you expect your people to display a sound work ethic, to work hard for positive outcomes. As we have seen, however, the top-performers also work smart. If you help your people develop, learn, and explore the limits of what's possible you will open their eyes, broaden their perspective and set the bar higher than perhaps it was ever set for you. Don't be uncomfortable that they may build muscles you don't have. Good leaders surround themselves with people who are better than they are. In doing so you will create a climate which encourages learning and enables smart working to thrive. You can never have a monopoly on wisdom; and, when the tough times come, having encouraged an environment where ideas and creativity are valued, you and those around you will be best placed to pull together and navigate the way through choppy waters.

The one thing that we can be sure of is that volatility, uncertainty, complexity and ambiguity are all here to stay. In that context, the role of the manager and leader as someone who expects behaviours which are congruent with an environment which is about working hard *and* working smart is crucial. Demand 'agile behaviours' in your people in order to best equip them to arrive at the Resilience Destination Belief, where challenge and adversity are simply a fact of life. Our study shows that inflexible behaviours, where the only way through the challenge is to work harder, result in less successful salespeople. Agile behaviours include the ability to ask for feedback, to learn and reappraise constantly, to operate through 'rule of thumb' and not to insist upon rigidity, to demonstrate well-developed emotional intelligence and to focus upon people and situations, not relying upon perceived expertise or processes.

We learned that stress can be both debilitating and beneficial. Surely the role of a good manager and leader is to be close enough to our people to recognize when the bad stress is taking over and to step in. Equally, ensuring that the right amount of 'good stress' is present means that we have a climate of competitiveness, of stretch and challenge and reasonable expectation. In summary, the question here is: how am I inculcating mind-sets and behaviours which will encourage my people to show innovative and creative thinking, manage their personal wellbeing and support others when resilience is called for?

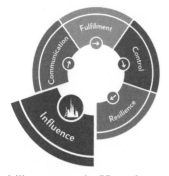

The Destination Belief for Influence is that *Successful people are influential*. As we have learned, some people prefer to follow a Journey Motivator focused upon influence through strength, while others prefer to adopt an influence through flexibility approach. How does a sales manager or leader affect the environment in such a way that both Journey Motivators are supported, but that the direction of travel towards the optimal balance gains momentum? One solution is to ensure that you create a culture of trust through shared values and motivation. Say what you'll do, then do what you say. Be consistent and fair in the way rewards and any necessary reprimands are meted out. Teach people when to stand firm, when to bend and when to say 'No'. Support their choices. Consider inviting your sales team to sign up to an agreed code of values that promotes an agreed standard for, amongst other things, integrity and honesty to each other, to the organization and to customers.

Take a scientific approach to motivation by understanding what motivates each of your team members and give them the boost they need to get it. They might crave knowledge, harmony, connections, a social benefit, power, achievement, accomplishment, and maybe even money. Some salespeople are motivated by being told of a high goal you don't believe they will achieve. They may do it just to prove you wrong. Re-read the opening chapter of The Salesperson's Secret Code and consider now how you might tap into the differing motivations of your people.

Walk the talk: be the very model of behaviour you expect of your salespeople. This means mastering the art of everything from storytelling, to demonstrating curiosity, to listening to your own personal resilience. This is no time to be a Gorilla and an exponent of Lightning. Walking the talk is about being that Guerrilla with a voice that rumbles like Thunder.

All the foregoing ideas send a clear message to your people. They observe and experience situations when you use your power, your 'gorilla talents'. They also notice those times when you adopt mind-sets and behaviours which demonstrate your ability to manage and lead situationally, with elegance and flexibility: these are your 'guerrilla talents'. In creating this environment you will demand certain behaviours, which will develop your people's capabilities. Once they believe that they have the talent (and value what it can do) they will be far more likely to become the exemplar salesperson you envision them to be.

The meaning of communication is the effect it has, not the intent or desire by which it is sent. This is another belief. If we hold it to be true it means that when we engage with our customers and our message is falling on stony ground, we don't push our message all the harder. We presuppose instead that there might be something we could do to better communicate and engage differently. In short, we stop trying to be the lightning that strikes twice and aim instead to be that rolling thunder which we noted made our top-performers more successful than others. The belief drives the behaviour. This is where the environment creat-ed by sales managers and leaders can have a major impact. Support the Communication Journey Motivators – expect your people to be able to communicate like lightning, to know their products and services inside out and to be able to state the various features and benefits; but also expect them to display the attributes of thunder sellers – listening, focusing on the customer, giving without expectation and so on. Is this the environment, the climate, you are sustain-ing for your team?

Most, if not all, managers understand that they should create a sales culture, outline the behaviours they require and develop the skills and talents of their people. What this study has shown is that the best managers will now align their activities in the directions of optimizing the intensi-ty of each of the Journey Motivators because in doing so they will lay the foundations for their teams' success. From the setting of a context for people to operate within, the expected behaviours become clear. For example, when a culture of positivity and challenge is in place people un-derstand that they are expected to behave in ways that sup-port that climate. The skills and talents they bring to bear are then aligned to the behaviours and the environment.

Managers and leaders will help their people unlock the secret code by going further. It was evident that many of the lower-performing salespeople in the study *believed* that they were doing the right things, thinking in the right way. The unfortunate truth is that many of these lower-per-formers are perfectly capable of performing at the level of the top-performers, but do not do so because they have not been challenged to think about what they believe and to recalibrate, or establish for the first time, a mind-set which we know will set them up for success. Managers who coach their people suddenly become invaluable. The conversations that unlock the secret code are less about lagging indicators – how many calls made last week, how many meetings held – and more about leading ones. "Tell me about the research you are doing on your customer before your meeting." "What do you think the customer will find most relevant about our offering?" "Why do you think that is?" "In what ways will you be pushing yourself to learn something new in the coming week?"

Now the salespeople are being challenged to operate at a level beyond behaviours and skills. They are being asked to think about why it might be important to research a customer, to think about why aligning their offering to the customer's needs is so important and to adopt a mind-set which says continuous self-improvement is desirable. "What is important about that?" and "Why does that matter?" are two questions which can be deployed to help identify the inner beliefs. Environmental, behavioural and skills-based questions are all very well; they help managers to understand what people do, where they do it, how they do it and so on. But the questions which are aimed at understanding inner beliefs are so crucial because this is where we gain insight into *why* people do what they do. As possessors of the secret code for sales success at the top level you are now armed with lots of questions which you can ask at the level of belief. Now, more than ever before, the need for managers and leaders to engage fully with their people and to discover what and why certain things are important to them, is self-evident.

One thing which becomes clear from this is that managers and leaders must be clear what they believe. After all, it's rather hard to coach someone in terms of adjusting their beliefs to align with the best-of-the-best if our own belief system is out of kilter. Don't forget, therefore, to spend an appropriate amount of time thinking about how you measure up to the Journey Motivator intensity balance of the top-performers. Look to your own behaviours and to your own management and leadership style. Are they aligned to everything we have discussed? Do they support the cracking of the salesperson's secret code or do they make it more inaccessible? In short, get your own house in order before fixing the roof on someone else's!

In the end, The Salesperson's Secret Code has helped to unlock the true sense of purpose and identity that the most successful salespeople in our study group possess. No one person is wholly identical to another, but what is apparent is that the top-performers see themselves as people who:

- Fear failure, but who use that fear to challenge themselves to be the best they can possibly be
- Don't dwell on what they cannot control, but instead make things happen to their own and their customers' benefit
- Work hard to get through tough times, but are always looking to manage their stress and the energy they expend through working smarter
- Know that they possess the power to influence others and temper this with a flexible approach in order to bring others with them
- Understand intimately their product or service offering and communicate their expertise appropriately through continuous and dynamic dialogue.

Those identity statements may have come from a study about the beliefs of successful salespeople, but they could just as easily apply to role-model leaders. Perhaps therein lies another truth – that the top-performing salespeople are also exemplar leaders.

In this book we have endeavoured to shine a light onto areas which we often prefer to keep hidden. Our beliefs are intensely personal things, but this study has sought to offer ways for anyone (be they in sales or not) to adopt a balance of beliefs which we observed leading to success time after time. In order to do so, some of us will necessarily have to dispense with our previous patterns of thought. For some this may prove more difficult than for others. There is an apocryphal story about the manager who had a graduate assigned to their team. This young high-flyer thought that they had all the bases covered, that this role was a tempo-rary stopping-off point on the way to the top. Despite this, they kept telling the manager that they were keen to learn, determined to benefit from the experience of others. On many occasions the manager sought to offer counsel, to mentor and to coach the ambitious young person, but time after time, these approaches were met with resistance.

One day the manager decided that enough was enough and when they met in the manager's office, the manager asked if the graduate would like a glass of water. A glass was placed in front of the graduate and the manager took a bottle of water and began to fill it. However, as the glass filled to the brim, the manager did not stop and water began to pour down the sides of the glass and over the desktop. All the papers on the desk, including those of the graduate, began to soak up the water and large amounts started to fall off the desk onto the floor. The graduate was shocked and angry, screaming, "Stop! You are mad and you are ruining everything, including all my work." But the manager just kept pouring water until the bottle was empty. Only in that moment, as the last drops left the bottle, did the manager speak. "You told me that you wanted water from my bottle. But if you want to collect my water you must keep your glass empty."

We can gain insight and revelation only when our minds are open to the possibility of change. When we refuse to be open we treat new insights as enemies that we need to repel. If we embrace new and endless possibilities, if we hold out an empty glass, we can allow new realities to pour into our lives.

Change begins with us, so figure out what the secret code means to you and then enjoy the challenge of filling the glasses of your people through the insights gained from our Iconics and the beliefs of the top 5% of salespeople. As iconic Piano Matchmaker, Erica Feidner said, "I don't really know what my secret code for success is, but now that I know it has been codified I can't wait to find out!"

APPENDIX
A

ALIGNMENT TO 6 ATTITUDES

Our original research in 2013 revealed a range of factors that motivated the 500 low-performing and 500 high-performing salespeople. In no specific order these were:

- A desire to learn, discover and grow.
- A desire to earn well for the effort they expend.
- A desire to experience personal wellbeing or self-actualization.
- A desire to be part of something with others and to help others through what they do.
- A desire to be in control of their own destiny and to enjoy recognition for their success.
- A desire to deliver to the best possible standard and to do things *in the right way*.

Our psychometricians soon pointed out that our data revealed a remarkable alignment with Eduard Spranger's research concerning values and attitudes. Spranger (1882–1963) was a German philosopher and psychologist who published *Types of Men*, a significant contribution to personality theory still widely used today[1].

We have, therefore, acknowledged Spranger's ongoing contribution to human understanding and built upon his model. We wish to add to current understanding rather than create a new model for its own sake. To us, this was serendipity.

We grouped the motivations in alignment with the Spranger 6 Attitudes (*see Figure 10*):

- Theoretical
- Utilitarian
- Aesthetic
- Social
- Individualistic
- Traditional

FIGURE 10
THE 6 ATTITUDES (MOTIVATORS)

It's worth taking a moment to understand this. People are multi-dimensional. Under most circumstances a person will follow one or two types of motivator by default.

Salespeople with a dominant **Theoretical** motivation seek knowledge for its own sake. They can process vast and diverse sources of information, see patterns quickly, and enjoy showing their intellectual prowess. But this breadth of knowledge may cause them to move from idea to idea, from fad to fad, without building much depth. Placed under pressure, their appetite to "be right" may become obsessive to the point that practical matters like safety, reputation, honesty, family or financial constraints are ignored. Should they be made responsible for turning theory into action, they prefer to recommend more study. Pressed further, they may try to foresee all contingencies, and catastrophize over what *might* be. It is not uncommon to see this type jump ship when colleagues expect them to be practitioners as well as theoreticians.

Salespeople with a dominant **Utilitarian** motivation are capitalists who seek what is useful or practical. They focus on gaining a return on investment for their time, activity or money by netting things out and getting to the bottom line. Their value to others rests in being creative in how they harness resources to achieve an economic gain with minimal waste. They get work done through others, but don't tend to make many friends – their alliances last only as long as those people offer utility to the immediate goal. Placed under pressure, they can become workaholics who expect others to keep the same hours and burn the midnight oil until pressures abate and the goal is attained. Should difficulties increase further, their utilitarian focus can shift from group welfare to self-preservation, with little concern for others as they objectively and surgically set their world to rights.

Salespeople with a dominant **Aesthetic** motivation seek new experiences and self-expression. Often non-conformists, they seek to experience new things – the more they experience, the more they evolve and the sharper their intuition becomes. Their value to others rests in their ability to grasp the big picture, see areas of conflict, empathize with people and creatively bring about course corrections. They commonly seek out seminars or experiences that offer personal growth. Placed under pressure (as in a chaotic or contentious environment), they have difficulty functioning, ignore the facts and make decisions based on how they *feel* things ought to be in an ideal world, not always as they really are.

Salespeople with a dominant **Social** motivation seek to eliminate conflict. They focus on how actions will benefit others, and invest their time to help others achieve their potential. Their value to others lies in their selflessness, generosity in how they apply their time and talents, and being a champion who rights wrongs. They are people-oriented more than profit-oriented, and want to contribute to a meaningful mission. Placed under pressure they can increase their zeal for achieving the mission at all costs, and go beyond the point where others would turn back from a lost cause. This can place people and resources at risk. If others resist, they can swing from being social to being dictatorial.

Salespeople with a dominant **Individualistic** motivation seek to assert themselves. They focus on advancement of position and power for themselves or their company. Their value to others rests in a Machiavellian capacity to plan the strategy and tactics needed for victory. They tend to seek out and surround themselves with material possessions and accoutrements that telegraph an inflated authority, for example premium brand watches, rings, pens, desks, suits, titles and awards. They cultivate alliances that help advance their position, but are capable of dropping them just as easily when no longer relevant. Placed under pressure (such as a real or perceived threat to their power and position, a carrot motivator being reneged on, or being placed in a position where advancement is unlikely), their instinct for self-preservation may outweigh other considerations. In the final analysis, the Individualistic salesperson wants success and wants recognition for that success.

Salespeople with a dominant **Traditional** motivation want to understand their meaning or role in the scheme of things, and seek structures to achieve goals "the right way." They apply the system they believe in to everyday matters and to business decisions. Their value to others rests in their dedication to "the system" – they are consistent in making value judgements, work "by the book" and are dutiful and loyal to the chain of command. They also hold others accountable to the standards they espouse, serving as a good conscience for any group. But they can hold on to tradition for too long, and don't always deal with change well. When facing pressure to change or opposing belief systems, they tend to be closed-minded, stick with what they know, and may even break new rules to preserve the old ones.

Figure 11 below shows on average how much of the time the six motivators were driving the behaviour of low-performing and high-performing salespeople.

Low Performers   High Performers

Low Performers	Motivator	High Performers
17.99%	Theoretical	18.29%
44.35%	Utilitarian	22.85%
4.60%	Aesthetic	11.64%
12.13%	Social	15.05%
15.90%	Individualistic	20.14%
5.02%	Traditional	12.04%

FIGURE 11
DISTRIBUTION OF SIX MOTIVATORS ACROSS LOW AND HIGH PERFORMERS

The most commonly occurring motivator in the lower-performing group (44.35%) is the Utilitarian motivator; this is about time spent versus reward gained, efficiency and perceived value derived. The next most prevalent motivator doesn't occur more than 17.99% of the time, nearly two thirds less frequently. This is noteworthy because Utilitarian values closely mirror the one-dimensional 1950s stereotype of salespeople pounding the streets and hustling buyers for business. That might have worked in the post-war industrial boom when product was king, but today, especially with a millennial generation seeking roles offering them meaning and purpose, this type of motivation, when over-extended, appears to drive weak sales behaviour and poor results.

During the research process, we wondered to what extent being motivated by time and money is a by-product of managers asking tactical pipeline review questions like, *How much selling-time did you have last week? How many calls did you fit in? How many are planned this week? How much money are they worth? What day will you sign them?* We found that while it probably doesn't help the sales profession evolve when managers keep assessing it against lagging indicators, the practice certainly doesn't impact people's core motivators. This validated that what we were finding were deeply held intrinsic motivations, not extrinsic, environmental affectations.

What stands out in the results of high performers is how the six motivations are distributed more evenly. Clearly these sellers had evolved a greater sense of fluency in how they respond to situations. This implies a degree of emotional mastery and maturity at work.

This insight raised more questions than it gave answers and so, in 2015, we began the research that has led to the discovery of the Salesperson's Secret Code.

THE CODE

BREAKERS

IAN MILLS is the Managing Partner of Transform Performance International, and a co-author of *100 Big Ideas to Help You Succeed* (LID, 2013). He has been a salesperson and led sales organizations in the fast-moving consumer goods, financial and technology sectors. Since 1999, Ian has been a leading light in the building of a globally successful performance improvement consultancy that has delivered solutions in over 60 countries. From Lima in the west to Beijing in the east, he has led behaviour change and transformation projects with corporations such as Hewlett-Packard, Deloitte and American Express.

MARK RIDLEY is a founding Partner of Transform Performance International and a driving force behind this highly successful UK-based firm. An inspirational coach and co-author of *100 Big Ideas to Help You Succeed* (LID, 2013), he has worked as a strategist, chair and facilitator with global brands, investment houses and academic institutions for over 25 years, in 60 countries, inspiring leadership and coaching talent, growing sales and transforming the way people communicate. He facilitates regularly at major conferences and events worldwide and is an acknowledged expert in sales leadership, emotional intelligence and collaborative excellence

DR BEN LAKER is a Partner at Transform Performance International and joined the firm following a research and academic career. He co-founded the Centre for High Performance and ran MBA programmes at the U.K.'s Kingston Business school. He was also a Visiting Professor at the Russian Presidential Academy of National Economy. Ben has worked with Apple and NASA, authored three Harvard Business Review articles on leadership and has been featured in *Forbes*, *The Economist*, *The Times*, *The Guardian*, *The Telegraph*, *The Independent* and on BBC Newsnight.

TIM CHAPMAN partners with Transform Performance International and is a Lecturer in Behavioural Economics and International Sales Management at the University of York. He has over 25 years' experience in international B2B sales, in a variety of front-line sales, senior management and sales excellence roles. He has built a successful sales consultancy and coaching business, Sales EQ, delivering projects to a range of blue chip and medium-sized companies in the UK, Europe, Canada and the USA.

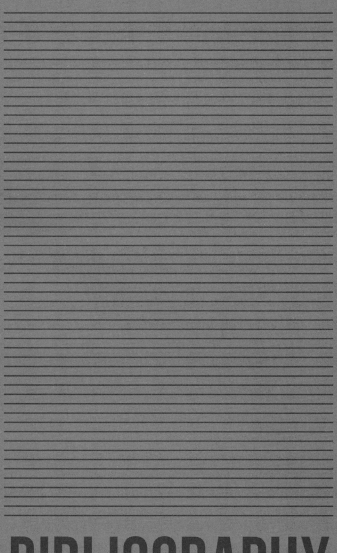

BIBLIOGRAPHY

1. Eduard Spranger, Types of Men: The Psychology & Ethics of Personality, (Halle: M. Niemeyer, 1928).

2. 'William E. Smith, "Disaster Screaming Like a Banshee," Time Magazine, 2001.

3. William Moulton Marston, Emotions of Normal People, (London: Cooper Press, 2014).

4. James Allen, As a Man Thinketh, (London: The Savoy Publishing Company, 1903).

5. Eliot Rosen and Ellen Burstyn, Experiencing the Soul: Before Birth, During Life, After Death, (London: Hay House Inc., 1998).

6. Matt Mayberry, "The Extraordinary Power of Visualizing Success," Entrepreneur Magazine, 30 January, 2015, accessed 20 October, 2016, https://www.entrepreneur.com/article/242373.

7. Denis Waitley, Seeds of Greatness – The Ten Best-Kept Secrets of Total Success, (New York, NY: Pocket Books, 2010).

8. Nathan Furr, "How Failure Taught Edison to Repeatedly Innovate," Forbes, 9 June, 2011, accessed 21 October, 2016, https://www.forbes.com/sites/nathanfurr/2011/06/09/how-failure-taught-edison-to-repeatedly-innovate/#3ab16eb865e9.

9. Nick Curtis, "Why Failing Upwards is the Best Way to Succeed," The Telegraph, 16 February, 2016, accessed 22 October, 2016, http://www.telegraph.co.uk/wellbeing/mood-and-mind/why-failing-upwards-is-the-best-way-to-succeed.

10. Jennifer Nielsen, "Highlights from Oprah's JK Rowling Interview," Jennielsen, 4 October, 2010, accessed 13 May, 2017, http://www.jennielsen.com/archives/501.

11. Ramin Assemi, "39 Shocking Sales Stats That Will Change the Way You Sell," Closeio, 6 November, 2015, accessed 23 October, 2016, http://blog.close.io/39-shocking-stats-that-will-change-the-way-you-sell.

12. Henry Charles Link, The New Psychology of Selling and Advertising (Whitefish, MT: Literary Licensing, 1932), 102.

13. Alex Hill, Liz Mellon, Ben Laker and Jules Goddard, "The one type of leader who can turn around a failing school" Harvard Business Review, October, 2016, accessed 21 October, 2017, https://hbr.org/2016/10/the-one-type-of-leader-who-can-turn-around-a-failing-school.

14. Carmine Gallo, Talk Like TED – The 9 Public Speaking Secrets of the World's Top Minds, (London: Pan Macmillan, 2014).

15. Abraham Maslow, A Theory of Human Motivation (New York, NY: Start Publishing, 2012), 46.

16. Helmuth Graf von Moltke, Moltke on the Art of War: Selected Writings, ed. Daniel J. Hughes, trans. Harry Bell, (Novato, CA: Presidio Press, 1996).

17. Mike Berardino, "Mike Tyson explains one of his most famous quotes," Sun Sentinel, 9 November, 2012, accessed 13 May, 2017, http://articles.sun-sentinel.com/2012-11-09/sports/sfl-mike-tyson-explains-one-of-his-most-famous-quotes-20121109_1_mike-tyson-undisputed-truth-famous-quotes.

18. Sigmund Freud, Das Unbehagen in der Kultur, (Wien: Internationaler Psychoanalytischer Verlag, 1930).

19. Oliver Wendell Holmes, The Complete Poetical Works of Oliver Wendell Holmes, (Boston, MA: Houghton, Mifflin and Company, 1908).

20. David Daniel Kennedy, Feng Shui for Dummies, 2nd ed. (Hoboken, NJ: John Wiley & Sons, 2010).

21. S. F. Scudder, "Sociological Systems," Communication Theory, 15 January, 2016, accessed 19 May, 2017, http://www.opentextbooks.org.hk/ditatopic/14729.

22. Richard Bach, Running from Safety: An Adventure of the Spirit, (New York, NY: Delta, 1995).

23. Post Staff Report, "Why Losers Have Delusions of Grandeur," New York Post, 23 May, 2010.

24. Charles Darwin, The Descent of Man: Selection in Relation to Sex, (London: John Murray Publishers, 1871).

25. Justin Kruger and David Dunning, "Unskilled and Unaware of It: How Difficulties in Recognizing One's Own Incompetence Lead to Inflated Self-Assessments," Journal of Personality and Social Psychology 77, (1999).

26. Marc Abrahams, "Those Who Can't, Don't Know It," Harvard Business Review, December, 2005, accessed 24 October, 2016, https://hbr.org/2005/12/those-who-cant-dont-know-it.

27. Confucius, The Analects of Confucius, trans. William Edward Soothill. (Yokohama: Fukuin Printing Company, 1910), 168.

28. A. H. Maslow, "A Theory of Human Motivation," Psychological Review 50, (1943): 370-396.

29. Kelly McGonigal, The Upside of Stress: Why Stress Is Good for You, and How to Get Good at It, (London: Penguin Random House, 2015).

30. Human Performance Institute, "Engagement is the keystone of employee productivity," Human Performance Institute national survey, February 2010, accessed 26 October, 2016, https://fisher.osu.edu/supplements/10/7951/Engagement%20White%20Paper.pdf

31. Ross Devol et al, The Economic Burden of Chronic Disease: Charting a New Course to Save Lives and Increase Productivity and Economic Growth, (Santa Monica, CA: Milken Institute, October 2007).

32. "At a Glance 2015," The National Center for Chronic Disease Prevention and Health Promotion (CDC), accessed 27 October, 2016, https://www.cdc.gov/chronicdisease/resources/publications/aag/pdf/2015/nccdphp-aag.pdf.

33. https://en.wikipedia.org/wiki/Death_of_a_Salesman#cite_note-2

34. Institute of Medicine, "PTSD Compensation and Military Service," National Research Council, September 2007, accessed 28 October, 2016, https://www.nap.edu/catalog/11870/ptsd-compensation-and-military-service.

35.   Randy Herring, "Recuperation and Muscular Growth!,"
      Bodybuilding, 22 July, 2016, accessed 2 November, 2016,
      https://www.bodybuilding.com/content/recuperation-and-
      muscular-growth.html.

36.   "Employee & Retiree Services," SAS Institute, accessed 4
      November, 2016, http://www.sas.com/corporate/sasfamily/
      extras/index.html#menus.

37.   "Fortune Rankings," SAS Institute, accessed 6 November, 2016,
      http://www.sas.com/news/preleases/FortuneRanking09.html.

38.   Addam Corre, "15 Great Motivational Quotes from Henry
      Ford," Life Daily, 27 November, 2014.

39.   Arthur Miller, "Death of a Salesman," Penguin Books,
      1 January, 1996.

40.   Tony Schwartz, "Mind Game," New York Magazine, 19
      November, 1990.

41.   Christopher Clarey, "Strange Habits of Successful Tennis
      Players," New York Times, 21 June, 2008.

42.   Paul LeFavor, US Army Special Forces Small Unit Tactics
      Handbook, (Fayetteville, NC: Blacksmith Publishing, 2013), 238.

43.   Chris Lang, 11 April 2011, comment on "What is the average
      conversion rate for an outbound telemarketing campaign?,"
      Quora, 11 April, 2011, accessed 8 November, 2016, https://
      www.quora.com/What-is-the-average-conversion-rate-for-an-
      outbound-telemarketing-campaign

44.   Andrea Johnson "Webinar Replay: Research from Harvard,
      MIT Pinpoints Hard Lead Conversion Lessons with Easy
      Solutions," B2B Marketing Zone, 25 July, 2011, accessed 9
      November, 2016, https://www.b2bleadblog.com/2011/07/
      insidesaleswebinarreplay.html.

45.   Kristie Lorette, "Facts & Figures on Telemarketing," Chron, 22
      June, 2016, accessed 10 November, 2016, http://smallbusiness.
      chron.com/figures-telemarketing-2206.html.

46.   Abby Ellin, "Resiliency: the Buzzword That Could Take Your Career to New Heights," Johnson & Johnson, 9 October, 2016, accessed 12 November, 2016, https://www.jnj.com/innovation/resilience-in-the-workplace-training-human-performance-institute.

47.   Robert M. Sapolsky, Why Zebras Don't get Ulcers, 3rd ed., (New York, NY: St Martin's Press, 2004).

48.   Lynette Ryals and Iain Davies, "Vision Statement: Do You Really Know Who Your Best Salespeople Are?," Harvard Business Review, December, 2010, accessed 14 November, 2016, https://hbr.org/2010/12/vision-statement-do-you-really-know-who-your-best-salespeople-are.

49.   Laurence Minsky and Keith A. Quesenberry, "How B2B Sales Can Benefit from Social Selling," Harvard Business Review, 10 November, 2016, accessed 16 November, 2016, https://hbr.org/2016/11/84-of-b2b-sales-start-with-a-referral-not-a-salesperson.

50.   Andy Hoar, "Death of a (B2B) Salesman," Forrester Research, 13 April, 2015, accessed 18 November, 2016, https://www.forrester.com/report/Death+Of+A+B2B+Salesman/-/E-RES122288

51.   Nicholas A.C. Read and Stephen J. Bistritz, Selling to the C-Suite: What Every Executive Wants You to Know About Successfully Selling to the Top, (New York, NY: McGrawHill Education, 2009).

52.   Neil Rackham, To Increase Sales, Change the Way You Sell, (Harvard Business Review, 2014).

53.   Jim Keenan and Barbara Giamanco, Social Media and Sales Quota, (Denver, CO and Atlanta, GA: A Sales Guy Consulting and Social Centered Selling, 2013).

54.   Ibid.

55.   Alex Hisaka, "5 B2B Buyer Preferences to Know," LinkedIn Sales Blog, 24 September, 2014, accessed 22 November, 2016, https://www.linkedin.com/pulse/5-b2b-buyer-preferences-know-alex-hisaka.

56. Kevan Lee, "The 29 Most Common Social Media Rules: Which Ones Are Real? Which Ones Are Breakable?," Buffer, 2 March, 2015, accessed 24 November, 2016, https://blog.bufferapp.com/social-media-rules-etiquette.

57. Maggie Hibma, "The Marketer's Guide to Proper Social Media Etiquette," Hubspot, 6 May, 2013, accessed 28 November, 2016, https://blog.hubspot.com/marketing/marketers-guide-proper-social-media-etiquette#sm.00005pr9d2eb7f8sqsz2cm3jmun05.

58. Jodi Parker, "Social Media Etiquette Guide," Tollfreeforwarding, 18 July, 2014, accessed 29 November, 2016, https://tollfreeforwarding.com/blog/social-media-etiquette-guide.

59. Rebekah Radice, "10 Golden Rules to Successful Social Media Marketing," 25 November, 2014, accessed 2 December, 2016, https://rebekahradice.com/golden-rules-successful-social-media-marketing.

60. Chris Brogan, "An Insider's Guide to Social Media Etiquette," Owner Media Group, 24 February, 2011, accessed 5 December, 2016, http://chrisbrogan.com/socialmediaetiquette.

61. Travis Balinas, "Social Media Etiquette for Business," Outbound Engine, 23 September, 2015, accessed 7 December, 2016, http://chrisbrogan.com/socialmediaetiquette.

62. The Routledge Companion to Marketing History, eds. D.G. Brian Jones and Mark Tadajewskim, (Abingdon: Routledge, 2016).

63. Laura Barnett, "Death of a Salesman: No More Door-to-Door Britannica," The Guardian, 14 March, 2012, accessed 9 December, 2016, https://www.theguardian.com/media/shortcuts/2012/mar/14/britannica-death-salesmen-door.

64. Paula Gorry, "The Journey of Direct Selling," Sales Initiative, 30 November, 2015, accessed 12 December, 2016, http://www.sales-initiative.com/toolbox/selling/the-journey-of-direct-selling.

65. Katt Savage, "It Really Sucks: A Kirby Vacuum Salesperson's Story," Schizophasic, 10 May, 2012, accessed 16 December, 2016, http://schizophasic.blogspot.co.uk/2012/05/it-reallysucks-kirby-vacuum.html

66. Rebekah Bernard, "Can You Fake Empathy Until It Becomes Real?," KevinMD.com, 13 September, 2015, accessed 2 January, 2017, http://www.kevinmd.com/blog/2015/09/can-you-fake-empathy-until-it-becomes-real.html.

67. Anthony Goh and Matthew Sullivan, "The Most Misunderstood Business Concept in China," Business Insider, 24 February, 2011, accessed 5 January, 2017, http://www.businessinsider.com/the-most-misunderstood-business-concept-in-china-2011-2?IR=T.

68. Robert Cialdini, Influence: The Psychology of Persuasion, (London: Harper Collins, 1984).

69. Aristotle, On Rhetoric, trans. George A. Kennedy, (Oxford: Oxford University Press, 2011).

70. Sean O'Neill, "Cold Calling Analysis: How Many No's to Get a Yes," Vendere Partners, 11 August, 2011, accessed 7 January, 2017, http://info.venderepartners.com/bid/66537/Cold-Calling-Analysis-How-Many-No-s-to-Get-a-Yes.

71. "Lightning Really Does Strike More Than Twice," NASA, accessed 8 January, 2017, https://www.nasa.gov/centers/goddard/news/topstory/2003/0107lightning.html.

72. Jeremy Miller, "3% Rule: Engage Customers Before They Need Your Services," Sticky Branding, 5 May, 2015, accessed 10 January, 2017, https://stickybranding.com/3-rule-engage-customers-before-they-need-your-services.

73. Gerhard Gschwandtner, "Are You at Risk of Being Replaced by Technology?," Selling Power, 3 August, 2010, accessed 12 January, 2017, http://blog.sellingpower.com/gg/2010/08/are-you-at-risk-of-being-replaced-by-technology-.html.

74. Christopher Davie et al, "Three Trends in Business-to-Business Sales", McKinsey & Company, May, 2010, accessed 15 January, 2017, http://www.mckinsey.com/business-functions/marketing-and-sales/our-insights/three-trends-in-business-to-business-sales.

75. Keith Rosen, "Effective Listener: It Ain't About You", Profit Builders, Retrieved 27 November 2016, accessed 18 January, 2017, http://www.profitbuilders.com/articles/communication/skills-to-becoming-the-most-effective-listener.php.

76. Robert Dilts & Judith DeLozier, NLP II – The Next Generation: Enriching the Study of the Structure of Subjective Experience, (Capitola, CA: Meta Publications, 2010)

77. Sue Knight, NLP at Work: The Essence of Excellence, 3rd edn., (London: Nicholas Brealey Publishing, 2009).

78. Winston Churchill, His Complete Speeches, 1897–1963: Vol. 4 (1922-1928), ed. Robert Rhodes James, (New York, NY: Chelsea House Publishers, 1974), 3706.

79. Ian Mills and Mark Ridley, 100 Big Ideas to Help You Succeed, (London: LID Publishing, 2013).

BOOK DESCRIPTION

This book is for any sales professional, or indeed anyone involved in the sales process of their company, who wants to learn the secrets of successful selling. It is based on 20,000 hours of comparative analyses across the spectrum of performance and interviews with some of the world's most iconic salespeople. They share their personal opinions and conclusions drawn from their experience at organizations including Adidas, Cisco, Clarify, Deloitte, GSK, JP Morgan, Microsoft, Oracle, Steinway & Co., and Vodafone. The authors present the most rigorous global evaluation of how salespeople behave and how they are driven. In doing so, they reveal the secret code behind consistent, high-level success in sales.

RESEARCHERS

Ian Mills, Mark Ridley, Ben Laker & Tim Chapman

AUTHOR BIO

The book is a collaboration between Ian Mills, Mark Ridley, Ben Laker and Tim Chapman from Transform Performance International. All of them have extensive global experience working in performance improvement, both from an academic and a practitioner perspective.

Visit: www.salespersons-secret-code.com

EDITORS

Mark Ridley, Ben Laker & Nicholas A.C. Read